# BIODIVERSITY & HUMAN RIGHTS



## The International Rules for the Protection of Biodiversity

Elli Louka

Transnational Publishers

Published and distributed by *Transnational Publishers, Inc.*
Ardsley Park
Science and Technology Center
410 Saw Mill River Road
Ardsley, NY 10502

Phone: 914-693-5100
Fax: 914-693-4430
E-mail: info@transnationalpubs.com
Web: www.transnationalpubs.com



**Library of Congress Cataloging-in-Publication Data**

Louka, Elli.
Biodiversity and human rights : the international rules for the protection of biodiversity / by Elli Louka.
p. cm.
ISBN 1-57105-226-7
1. Biological diversity conservation. 2. Human rights. 1. Title.

QH75 .L675 2002
333.95'16'0973—dc21

2002023616



Manufactured in the United States of America

To SMF

# Acknowledgments

Many thanks to my teacher, Michael Reisman, for his support, and to my teacher at Wharton, Marshall Blume, for teaching me everything I know about the markets. Many thanks also to David Mair for his friendship and optimism.

# Contents

## Chapter 2
## Evaluation of Biodiversity Protection Methods



## Chapter 3
## International Rules for National Conservation



## Chapter 4
## International Rules for the Exchange of Germplasm

# List of Abbreviations

| | |
|---|---|
| AAA | American Anthropological Association |
| CAMPFIRE | Communal Area Management Programme for Indigenous Resources |
| CBC | Committee of Board Chairs |
| CBNRM | Community-Based Natural Resources Management |
| CDC | Center Directors Committee |
| CGIAR | Consultative Group on International Agricultural Research |
| CIAT | International Center for Tropical Agriculture |
| CIFOR | Center for International Forestry Research |
| CIMMYT | International Maize and Wheat Improvement Center |
| CIP | International Potato Center |
| CITES | Convention on the International Trade in Endangered Species of Wild Flora and Fauna |
| EECONET | European Ecological Network |
| EIA | Environmental Impact Assessment |
| FAO | Food and Agriculture Organization |
| GEF | Global Environment Facility |
| IARCs | International Agricultural Research Centers |
| IBPGR | International Board of Plant Genetic Resources |
| ICARDA | International Center for Agricultural Research in Dry Areas |
| ICRAF | International Center for Research in Agroforestry |
| ICRISAT | International Crops Research Institute for the Semi-Arid Tropics |
| IDRC | International Development Research Center |
| IFPRI | International Food Policy Research Institute |
| IITA | International Institute for Tropical Agriculture |
| ILM | International Legal Materials |

| | |
|---|---|
| ILO | International Labor Organization |
| ILRI | International Livestock Research Institute |
| IPGRI | International Plant Genetic Resources Institute |
| IRRI | International Rice Research Institute |
| ISNAR | International Service for National Agricultural Research |
| ITTO | International Tropical Timber Organization |
| IUCN | International Union for the Conservation of Nature |
| MTAs | Material Transfer Agreements |
| NARS | National Agricultural Research Systems |
| NEFs | National Environmental Funds |
| NGOs | Non-governmental Organizations |
| NSSL | National Seed Storage Laboratory |
| OAU | Organization of African Unity |
| ODA | Official Development Assistance |
| OECD | Organization for Economic Co-operation and Development |
| PVPA | Plant Variety Protection Act |
| RAFI | Rural Advancement Foundation International |
| SBSTTA | Subsidiary Body on Scientific Technical and Technological Advice |
| TAC | Technical Advisory Committee |
| TRIPs | Trade Related Intellectual Property Rights |
| UN | United Nations |
| UNCED | United Nations Conference for Environment and Development |
| UNDP | United Nations Development Programme |
| UNEP | United Nations Environment Programme |
| UNESCO | United Nations Educational Scientific, and Cultural Organization |
| UPOV | International Union for the Protection of New Varieties of Plants |
| WARDA | West Africa Rice Development Organization |
| WTO | World Tourism Organization |
| WWF | World Wildlife Fund for Nature |

# Introduction

Today many people believe that species are becoming extinct at an alarming rate because of forest destruction[1] and other consumptive uses of the biosphere. And this extinction continues despite the efforts, propelled by the Convention on Biological Diversity, to stem biodiversity loss.[2] Because of this alleged dramatic species loss international policies and rules have been developed to protect and preserve biodiversity. These policies, though, are frequently misguided because they are based on:

(1) static notions of what biodiversity is;
(2) conflicting feelings about the people who make a living out of it;
(3) nationalistic tendencies of control over biodiversity resources;
(4) trade prohibitions and restrictions that have rendered wildlife a rare resource traded illegally in black markets.

Current policies on biodiversity are based on notions that biodiversity is "static," something that needs to be "preserved" as it is. The people who live around biodiversity resources are either viewed as indigenous people who need to be protected or as local people who need to be punished for what is viewed as their destruction of biodiversity resources. The center of these policies is "saving" biodiversity with emphasis on "preservation" or "conservation"[3] rather than on ecosystem evolution and management.

---

1 Anecdotal evidence of forest destruction is burgeoning especially in developing countries. Lately the Food and Agriculture Organization (FAO) has claimed that deforestation is abating. The FAO claims a slowdown of 20 percent compared with the deforestation rate measured in the first half of the decade, *see* FAO, *The Global Forest Resources Assessment 2000* (2001). Many non-governmental organizations have disputed the claim since the FAO figures are based on the combined calculation of forests and plantations. If plantations are excluded from consideration, natural forests in the tropics are disappearing at a rate of 16 million hectares a year, *see* Emily Matthews, *Understanding the Forest Resources Assessment 2000* (2001).

2 *The Root Causes of Biodiversity Loss* 2 (Alexander Wood et al. eds., 2000).

3 Conservation implies the sound management of biodiversity given the existing

Even the recently adopted Biodiversity Convention is based on the conservation of biodiversity resources with emphasis on *in situ* conservation and national measures rather than local management, restoration or gene bank development. While the convention takes into account the needs of indigenous people and local people, it has yet to evolve into the instrument that would protect the rights of people as a means to biodiversity protection.

The alleged widespread species loss has led also to the adoption of mechanisms that prohibit or restrict the trade in endangered species. These restrictions and prohibitions rest on the rationale that if the trade in endangered species is outlawed, endangered species will be saved. However, engrained beliefs about the medicinal properties of or the status associated with products obtained from endangered species fuel demand and have created a black market that has enriched politicians and elites in developing countries. In the meantime, the poachers who operate on the ground—frequently poor farmers enticed to the trade because of the profits involved—are killed, tortured or jailed.

This study proposes a fundamental review of the international biodiversity protection policies. Instead of conservation/preservation, this study proposes to shift attention to ecosystem management with human dignity at the center of biodiversity protection. The human rights violations that conservation often entails have been reported in previous studies. Many studies have recommended a view of biodiversity that is dynamic and centers on the evolution of ecosystems rather than the preservation of biodiversity resources. In these studies it is recommended that the needs of people who live close to protected areas must be taken into account when designing conservation policies.[4] Without

---

social and economic constraints. Conservation supports the management of the ecosystem to produce goods and services for humans without depleting diversity and acknowledges the dynamic character of the ecosystems. Preservation, on the other hand, implies the protection of species and natural areas without taking into consideration human needs. *See* Donald Show, *Inside the Environmental Movement* 12–14 (1992). In this study the terms "conservation" and "preservation" are used interchangeably since the pursuit of conservation in many areas of the developing world has produced results similar to those advocated by preservation.

4 *See, e.g.*, bibliography cited in Chapter 1, Section 3.3.2.

formal requirements and standards, though, such recommendations have fallen on deaf ears. This study establishes human rights standards as the threshold standards for biodiversity protection, and by doing so it seeks to formalize and standardize the requirement that human needs and aspirations must be incorporated into conservation goals and policies. This study goes one step further: it recommends that conservation policies should not be adopted unless basic human rights requirements are satisfied.

Overall, the purpose of this study is twofold:

(1) To establish human rights standards as the core standards of biodiversity protection.
(2) To propose a comprehensive system of international rules for the protection of biodiversity. (For the components of this system and how it compares with the current system, *see* Table 1.) Today most international rules on biodiversity protection center on what each individual state can do to protect biodiversity. This study proposes that certain aspects of biodiversity protection could benefit from the development of a coherent system of international policymaking. Such aspects include wildlife trade, gene bank development and the transnational transfers of plant genetic resources.

The international system proposed here is based on the premise that restrictions or prohibitions are a poor way to salvage endangered wildlife. On the contrary, policies must be developed that would allow people to generate direct monetary profits from the wildlife. If wildlife continues to be perceived as a rare resource that cannot be traded freely, the illegal trade will persist. But if wildlife becomes a commodity traded legally in international markets, illegal behavior will have to subside.[5] Privatizing the management of endangered species for their products can motivate people to change their behavior and protect species otherwise considered unprofitable and thus dispensable.

---

[5] In today's regulated markets the initial lifting of a ban on the trading of a species or a product is likely to increase illegal behavior. But as the legal supplies of products start to meet the demand, the prices will stabilize minimizing speculative and illegal behavior.

**Table 1: National Biodiversity Management versus International Biodiversity Management**

| *National Biodiversity Management* | *International Biodiversity Management* |
|---|---|
| *Assumptions*<br>• Biodiversity as something *static*<br>• Ecosystem *preservation*<br>• Biodiversity loss as *extinction*<br>• Biodiversity is best managed *locally* | *Assumptions*<br>• Biodiversity as something *dynamic*<br>• Ecosystem *management*<br>• Biodiversity loss as *conversion*<br>• Biodiversity is best managed *locally but* the international system can provide standards (human rights) and incentives (free trade) that support local management |
| *Rationale*<br>• Protect biodiversity for its intrinsic value | *Rationale*<br>• Protect biodiversity because it serves human needs |
| *Policies for management*<br>• Top-down national management standards<br>• Lack of human rights standards | *Policies for management*<br>• National and international guidelines applied locally<br>• Human rights standards as threshold standards |
| • Incentives based on:<br>— non-consumptive uses of biodiversity<br>• Disincentives based on:<br>— national wildlife management and control<br>— insecure land tenure<br>— prohibitions and restrictions on the trade in wildlife<br>• National/regional management of protected areas | • Incentives based on:<br>— all profitable uses<br><br><br>— local wildlife management and control<br>— secure land tenure<br>— international free trade in wildlife<br>• International/regional/national management of landscapes/ conservancies |
| *Policies for access to genetic resources*<br>• Bilateral and multilateral arrangements for access to plant genetic resources | *Policies for access to genetic resources*<br>• A Multilateral System of regulated free access to all plant genetic resources |
| • National gene bank management | • International gene bank management |
| *Implementation Procedures*<br>• Strict enforcement through human rights violations | *Implementation Procedures*<br>• Self-enforcement and respect for human rights |

Because biodiversity resources could occasionally become lucrative, developing states have asserted physical control over biodiversity resources residing within their territory. Today to get access to those resources, companies must obtain first the prior consent of the state. Countries are attempting also to impose restrictions on the free transfer of material located in national and international gene banks and especially the material located in the International Agricultural Research Centers. This bureaucratic system that is surrounding the transfer of biodiversity resources has hampered innovation. It is proposed here that, in order to encourage experimentation with biodiversity resources of unknown use, an effort must be made to ensure as much as possible unencumbered access to those resources. Unencumbered access, as analyzed in Chapter 4, is not equivalent to uninhibited free access but it is access free of the bureaucracy encountered in many national systems today. For resources of known use located in international gene banks, controls may eventually have no material effect since most of these resources are duplicated in national gene banks. A restrictive international system, however, will make transfers of known, useful germplasm cumbersome, will create uncertainties, propel litigation, and stifle innovation. While today's politics would litigate against free access—the informal system that made possible the green revolution—*regulated* free access must be asserted to ensure that agricultural innovation will continue well into the future.

Regulated free access to resources will be facilitated if the International Agricultural Research Centers evolve into international institutions whose mandate will be the protection, experimentation and collection of germplasm for research purposes. As long as the International Agricultural Research Centers retain their ambiguous status, disputes will erupt about the resources they maintain. The International Agricultural Research Centers should be devoted to the international management of gene banks, provide assistance for the national gene bank programs of developing countries, and freely collect, preserve and disseminate germplasm to private or public entities that would like to experiment with it. This study supports also the proliferation and streamlining of international gene banks. International gene banks benefit from the economies of scale put together by many states. Because they are supported by the broader international community, international gene banks are essential for the protection of biodiversity.

The transnational management of transboundary resources is proposed here as a component of the international system for biodiversity protection. Many of the protected areas today straddle national frontiers, and they would benefit if the countries involved would cooperate constructively in their management. Such cooperation exists today in some parts of the world, but it is in many cases nominal and a far cry from an actual co-management of the resource. Also many transnational management efforts do not incorporate human dignity values and are focused on the management of "pure protected areas" rather than the management of inhabited landscapes. Community-based management or private conservancies based on the communal/private control of wildlife resources and secure land tenure are still national efforts to protect biodiversity and serve human needs. This study supports the international application of such efforts as a means to change the current model of conservation that implies the subordination of human needs to conservation goals.

To summarize, human rights, free trade in wildlife, transboundary management of transnational resources, international gene bank management guaranteed by regulated free access are proposed here as the cornerstone of an international policy for biodiversity management (*see* Figure 1). International biodiversity management does not mean that the details of biodiversity protection will be managed internationally. It means that the international system will use all of its tools including human rights instruments and free trade mechanisms to provide the guidance and incentives needed so that the local management of biodiversity resources can succeed. The international system could help resolve many of the issues involved in the management of transboundary resources and in the management of gene banks worldwide. International biodiversity management, as proposed here, may not achieve to "save" all biodiversity as it exists today. International biodiversity management can, however, help to maintain productive ecosystems, "save" many of the admired species, ensure agricultural innovation, and most of all contribute to the betterment of the lives of the poor of the developing world by treating them with the dignity they deserve.

**Figure 1: International Biodiversity Management**

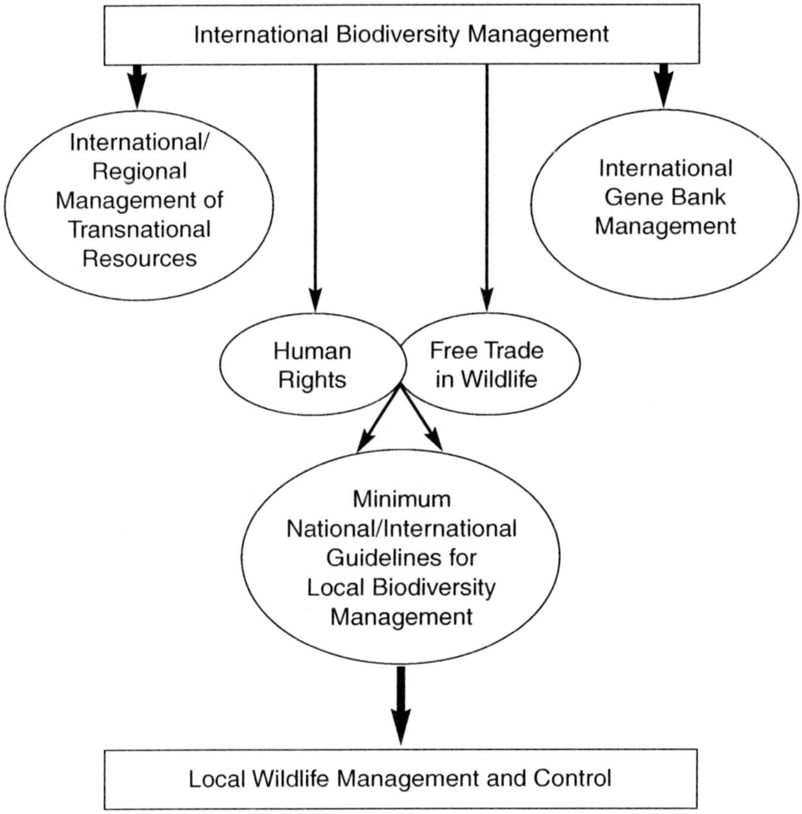


This book concentrates on the terrestrial biodiversity resources in developing countries and attempts to answer the question: what are the international policies needed to protect biodiversity without compromising human dignity and human rights values? Before prescribing such polices this study examines the prevalent definitions of biodiversity and the rationales that have been put forward for protecting it.

More specifically, Chapter 1 expands on the central claim of this study that biodiversity protection is dynamic and that it must include ecosystem management and restoration. Human dignity must be at the core of biodiversity protection. Chapter 1 defines biodiversity as ecosystem evolution and biodiversity loss as ecosystem conversion rather than ecosystem destruction. Chapter 1 proposes a new rationale for the protection of biodiversity, namely human dignity, and establishes human rights standards as the threshold standards for biodiversity protection. Chapter 1 examines the causes of biodiversity conversion and proposes minimum management standards that as a supplement to human rights standards provide the framework for the local management of biodiversity resources. Chapter 1 further analyzes the premises for the transnational management of transboundary resources and international gene bank development.

Chapter 2 examines the current available empirical evidence on the application of conservation methods and analyzes the current management options for biodiversity protection. Chapter 2 demonstrates that the conflicts between conservation and human rights make strict nature reserves unsustainable and privatization, restoration and gene bank development the preferable methods of biodiversity protection.

Chapter 3 examines the international instruments of conservation, including the Convention on the International Trade in Endangered Species of Wild Flora and Fauna (CITES) and the Convention on Biological Diversity. Chapter 3 examines the reasons behind the inability of these instruments to stem biodiversity conversion.

Chapter 4 examines the property rights over natural and genetic resources including physical control over biodiversity resources and the assertion of intellectual property rights over the modification of biodiversity resources. Chapter 4 analyzes the Convention on Biological Diversity and the Treaty on Plant Genetic Resources for Food and Agriculture and proposes regulated free access as the best system for the transfer and exchange of germplasm resources.

# Chapter 1
# Human Dignity as the Standard for International Biodiversity Management

## 1. CURRENT INTERNATIONAL POLICIES

### 1.1. The Lack of Human Dignity Standards

Many developing states have adopted strict laws for the protection of biodiversity that exclude people from biodiversity-rich areas and prohibit any sort of consumptive use in these areas. The enforcement of these laws depends on how much there is at stake in terms of the benefits brought by biodiversity protection and the costs of enforcement measures.

Developing countries that do not experience direct monetary benefits from biodiversity protection hardly enforce domestic regulations.

Developing countries who benefit from biodiversity because of a flourishing wildlife industry (including ecotourism, mass tourism and safari hunting)[1] enforce regulations depending on the amount of resources they have for enforcement. When the resources are abundant strict enforcement is the norm. Strict enforcement is necessary because, as explained below, most of the benefits from biodiversity protection do not trickle down to the people who live around biodiversity-rich areas and who break biodiversity protection laws to be able to survive. Strict and inhumane enforcement is an indispensable component of biodiversity protection policies in many developing countries.

The rhetoric of developed countries is also replete with references to strict enforcement in the nature reserves of the developing world. Even in studies that focus on reconciling human use and conservation, strict enforcement is proposed against "the intruders" of reserves. In a study sponsored by the World Bank, the World Wildlife Fund and the United

---

[1] Wildlife's importance as an economic commodity is prevalent in Africa where revenues from safari hunting and tourism often supplement revenues from agriculture and copper mining. *See* Clark C. Gibson, *Politicians and Poachers: The Political Economy of Wildlife Policy in Africa* (1999).

States Agency for International Development it is mentioned that: "There is always likely to be a conflict of interest between rural people's ability to earn a living and the management of nearby protected areas. It is unrealistic to assume that resource-poor people, living next to what may appear to them to be limitless resources of land . . . will readily support conservation ideas . . . conflicts cannot be expected to disappear, and the general need for strict enforcement appears inescapable."[2]

Strict enforcement has been legitimized by the practices of international institutions including the World Bank.[3] The World Bank has adopted a series of progressive policies aimed at protecting the rights of indigenous peoples. However, many of these policies have not been implemented. Many indigenous groups are still evicted from protected areas as a result of eco-development projects supported by the World Bank.[4] In a World Bank internal review it was found that only 15 out of 33 projects commissioned by the World Bank had taken into account the policies prescribed for the benefit of indigenous peoples.[5]

---

2 Michael Wells & Kartina Brandon, *People and Parks: Linking Protected Area Management with Local Communities* 47 (World Bank, World Wildlife Fund & U.S. Agency for International Development eds., 1992).

3 In 1982, the World Bank adopted guidelines on "Tribal People in Bank-Financed Projects." Despite the adoption of the policy, indigenous peoples are still adversely affected by the World Bank policies. In 1987, the World Bank adopted a new policy the purpose of which was to ensure "that indigenous peoples do not suffer adverse effects during the development process . . . and that they receive culturally compatible social and economic benefits." The policy promoted participation of indigenous peoples in project design and implementation, land tenure and resource security. But again in 1997 it was found that only 19 out of 48 projects attempted to address indigenous peoples needs as prescribed by the World Bank. Since 1998, the World Bank has been revising its indigenous peoples' policies with more emphasis on "self-development" and poverty alleviation. *See* Thomas Griffiths & Marcus Colchester, *Indigenous Peoples, Forests and the World Bank: Policies and Practice* 5–8 (Draft Discussion Document, Workshop on Indigenous Peoples, Forests and the World Bank, May 9–10, 2000).

4 *See* Chapter 2, Section 1.1.

5 *See supra* note 3, at 10.

Developed countries occasionally provide unilaterally the financial support to developing countries to ensure that environmental regulations are strictly enforced. But the intensity of support rendered by developed countries hedges on a number of factors. Terrorism, natural disasters and economic downturns often crowd the agendas of states and detract attention from environmental issues. Financial support for the strict enforcement of environmental laws is often lacking because "saving biodiversity" is not at the top of the agenda of many states. Many states believe that all the biodiversity needed for human purposes is already locked in in their national gene banks.

Strict enforcement, when applied in developing countries, often involves violent evictions of local people from conservation areas and shoot-to-kill policies. Kenya, for instance, has responded to the elephant poaching by ordering on-sight killing of poachers.[6] Poachers are often portrayed as hard-core criminals while, in reality, those who operate on the ground are often small farmers trying to make a living. What is surprising is that shoot-to-kill policies and large-scale evictions have been applauded and materially supported by groups who view them as the last resort measure in their battle to save nature. The World Wide Fund (WWF) provided Zimbabwe with the funds to buy a helicopter for its anti-poaching war. Deploying the helicopter, Zimbabwean soldiers killed more than fifty suspected poachers.[7] International donors, as an exchange for their contributions to preservation, have demanded the evictions of local populations. During the 1988 eviction of Maasai from the Mkomazi Game Reserve in Tanzania, the park's rangers burnt homes and destroyed property and livestock.[8] In 2000, the Bushmen from the Kalahari Desert in Botswana have been beaten and tortured because of hunting. Forced evictions ended officially in 1998 but the authorities do not view favorably the resettlement of Bushmen in their reserve. In

---

[6] For more details on Kenya's enforcement, *see* Chapter 2, Section 1.1.

[7] Raymond Bonner, *At the Hand of Man: Peril and Hope for Africa's Wildlife* (1993).

[8] Chief Edward Mbarmoti, "Mkomazi Game Reserve Now a 'Zoo,'" *Econews Africa*, Volume 5, Number 9, May 2, 1996.

March 2001, the local council stopped the provision of health care services, food and water to the villages in the reserve.[9]

Despite these egregious human rights violations, further details of which are provided in Chapter 2,[10] none of the international biodiversity protection instruments establishes human right standards as the threshold standards of biodiversity protection. Even the most recent biodiversity protection instruments, including the Convention on Biological Diversity, while they refer to the problems of poverty in the developing world and acknowledge the contributions of indigenous peoples to biodiversity,[11] are silent with regard to biodiversity protection in terms of human dignity values.

## 1.2. Emphasis on National Management Standards

In order to stem biodiversity conversion, countries have established national standards and adopted international guidelines. But monitoring and enforcement of standards are extremely limited when it comes to biodiversity protection. Who could possibly monitor and enforce regulations in a consistent and effective way in vast areas of treacherous land such as a tropical rainforest? Unless significant financial resources are committed, most monitoring and enforcement will produce far less than optimal results. Some countries may decide that strict enforcement is not in their best interests while others may decide that the benefits from biodiversity protection exceed the costs of enforcement and may do whatever is needed to enforce environmental laws including violating human rights. However, even, in this latter case, enforcement is rarely pervasive enough to deter people desperate to survive.

Many international and national rules have concentrated on the development of logging standards. Standards for logging are especially important because logging *per se*, while the cause of primary forest

---

9 "Botswana-Bushmen Tortured for Hunting," *Survival International Bulletin*, May 2001, available online at *http://www.survival.org.uk/bushmanuab0105.htm*.

10 Chapter 2, Section 1.1.

11 *See* Chapter 3, Section 2.

clearance, is not the cause of deforestation and biodiversity loss.[12] After the original removal, if the land is left undisturbed, regrowth can be quick. Also soil erosion is unlikely to happen if the right logging techniques are applied.[13]

Most sound logging techniques, though, are not applied consistently. Some of them are considered impractical and costly at least in the short-term.[14] Companies with limited concession agreements do not have the incentives to assist in maintaining the productivity of forested land beyond their tenure.[15] Untrained workers, left without supervision, are reluctant to apply more complex harvesting techniques.[16] And governments do not simply have the resources to monitor the implementation of national legislation and all concession agreements.

---

12 *See infra* Section 3.3.2.

13 Methods to avoid unnecessary forest destruction include: avoiding the use of heavy machinery, use of balloon and helicopter instead of road transportation for harvested wood, road reduction and revegetation, keeping logs off the ground, maintenance of litter layer and understory vegetation, buffer zones around stream channels. *See* Jack Westoby, *Introduction to World Forestry* 157 (1989); L.S. Hamilton & A.J. Pearce, "Soil and Water Impact of Deforestation," in *Deforestation: Social Dynamics in Watersheds and Mountain Ecosystems* 75 (J. Ives & D.C. Pitt eds., 1988); *Conservation of Genetic Resources in Tropical Forest Management* 26 (FAO Paper 107 ed., 1993). *See also* John Wyatt-Smith, "Problems and Prospects for Natural Management of Tropical Moist Forests," in *Natural Management of Tropical Moist Forests* 5, 13 (Francois Mergen & Jeffrey R. Vincent eds., 1987).

14 Hamilton & Pearce, *id.* at 88. *See also* A. Gõmez-Pompa & F.W. Burley, "The Management of Tropical Natural Forests," in *Rain Forest Regeneration and Management* 3, 15 (A. Gõmez-Pompa, T.C. Whitmore & M. Hadley eds., 1991).

15 For example, concessions in Asia are granted for periods of 21–25 years, even though the minimum realistic felling cycle is 30–35 years and the rotation is 60–70 years. Concession size and duration are very important in maintaining sustainable forest management. However, most of the time concessions granted are too small in size and duration and the concessionaires have no incentives to care about the future productivity of the land. *See* E. Barbier et al., *Economic Linkages Between Trade in Tropical Timber and the Sustainable Development of Forests* 48 (Final Report, International Institute for Environment and Development ed., 1993).

16 Wyatt-Smith, *supra* note 13, at 14.

International policymaking on logging standards has been helpful in giving guidance on what good logging practices are,[17] but it is followed rarely by monitoring and enforcement. Since the damage to the soil and the forest has to do more with forest management on the ground rather than with the quantity of timber removed, monitoring becomes even more crucial.[18] The difficulty of imposing and enforcing logging standards shows how difficult it is to impose standards for agriculture and grazing.[19] Agriculture and grazing are much more fragmented activities and are performed by millions of households rather than by a few large companies. Unless these households decide that it is in their best interests to comply, biodiversity conversion will continue as usual even in the face of strict enforcement. As mentioned above, enforcement measures, no matter how drastic they are, can rarely curb the will of people who see the violation of the law as their only means to survival.

---

[17] *See ITTO Guidelines for the Sustainable Management of Natural Tropical Forests* (ITTO Policy Development Series 1 ed., 1992).

[18] *See* Caroline Sargent & M. Lowcock, "Options for the Coordination of International Action in Forest Conservation and Management," in *Technical Workshop to Explore Options for Global Forestry Management* 153 (David Howlette & Caroline Sargent eds., 1991).

[19] Today farmers are encouraged to adopt what is called "sustainable agriculture." Sustainable agriculture involves, *inter alia:*

- soil conservation—many farmers combat soil erosion by non-till farming;
- conservation tillage and other techniques;
- sound management of water supply and use;
- avoidance of the salinization and contamination of water by pesticides;
- reduction of air pollution (which includes smoke from agricultural burning and nitrous oxide emissions from the use of nitrogen fertilizer).

The most adverse environmental impacts associated with grazing can be mitigated by applying the appropriate grazing system. The application of the appropriate grazing system means that: first, the number of stock per unit area (stocking rate) must be correct for the landscape and the forage resources; second, the long-term carrying capacity of the stocking rate must take into account short and long-term droughts; third, the manager must achieve sufficient control to reduce the overuse of some areas and the underuse of other areas. *See* Gail Feenstra et al., *What Is Sustainable Agriculture?* (UC Sustainable Agriculture Research and Education Program, University of California, Davis, December 1997), available online at *http://www.sarep.ucdavis.edu/concept.htm*.

## 1.3. Prohibitions and Restrictions on Wildlife Trade as a Disincentive for Local Management

Most commodities in the world today are freely traded. But the same is not true with wildlife. Wildlife trade is greatly restricted or prohibited by the CITES Convention. While international institutions generally support the South-to-North trade in agricultural products, the trade in wildlife is heavily controlled. According to some commentators, free trade is propagated by the developed world as means to increase productivity, but when it comes to free trade in wildlife—a commodity in which the developing world enjoys a competitive advantage—the trade becomes restrictive.[20]

Free trade in wildlife is not supported because, according to the prevailing view, wildlife is not a commodity. Most of wildlife resources, according to some estimates, are on the verge of extinction. If this is true they could hardly be categorized as commodities and they need to be protected. The CITES Convention restricts/bans the trade in wildlife to achieve exactly that: its protection.

But, as will be seen below, the restrictions and prohibitions have created illegal markets in which wildlife is traded.[21] Restrictions and prohibitions have undermined also local wildlife management systems that, if pursued under a free trade regime, could provide significant wealth for many people in developing countries.

## 1.4. Transnational Protected Areas

The only means of international biodiversity management supported by the current international system is that of the development of transnational protected areas. As analyzed in Chapter 3, many treaties support the efforts of states to develop and manage collectively their protected areas. The possibilities of the transnational management of protected areas are bountiful given the number of protected areas that are shared

---

20 Marshall Murphree, "Rural Poverty, Democracy and Wildlife Conservation," available online at *http://wildnetafrica.co.za/cites/info/vfs_essay_001.html*.

21 *See* Chapter 2, Section 1.2.

across borders and the economies of scale that can be taken advantage of in the management of such areas.[22]

Today efforts to create transnational parks involve informal/grass roots liaisons or formal agreements that take the shape of joint declarations, memoranda of agreement, or letters of intention. While formal agreements are the strongest basis for the establishment of joint protected areas, grass-roots cooperation is needed for the everyday smooth functioning of a transnational area.

One of the most ambitious efforts to manage biodiversity transnationally involves the agreement signed in 2000 by South Africa, Zimbabwe and Mozambique. The purpose of the agreement is to create a cross-border conservation park managed by a transnational authority to promote biodiversity protection and ecotourism in the region. The effort is ambitious because the parties to the agreement are of unequal economic power and obstacles remain such as that of controlling Mozambique's population as it tries to infiltrate South Africa through the park and poaching in both Zimbabwe and Mozambique.[23]

Other efforts include: transboundary collaboration between the United States and Mexico along the United States-Mexican border,[24] the tri-state project between the Central African Republic, Congo and Cameroon[25]

---

22 Dorothy C. Zbicz, *Transfrontier Ecosystems and Internationally Adjoining Protected Areas* (1999) (for instance, 136 clusters of contiguous protected areas have been identified. All these clusters contain 488 individual protected areas and involve 98 different countries almost half of the world's 224 countries and dependent territories. Each cluster is comprised by at least two protected areas. Some clusters contain up to thirteen protected areas).

23 "S. Africa, Neighbors Sign Cross-Border Park Pact," *Reuters News Service*, Nov. 13, 2000, available online at *http://www.reuters.com*.

24 José Cisneros, "Transboundary Collaboration in the Protection of Shared Natural Resources along the United States-Mexico Border," in *Parks for Peace* 61 (International Conference on Transboundary Protected Areas as a Vehicle for International Co-operation, September 1997, Conference Proceedings, Draft of 30 Jan. 1998).

25 Steve Gartland, "The Central African Experience in Transfrontier Protected Areas. A Case Study of the Tri-State Project Between the Central African Republic, Congo, Cameroon; and the National Parks between Cameroon and Nigeria," in *Parks for Peace*, *id*. at 242.

and the transfrontier reserve on the Korean Peninsula.[26] Efforts in support of transnational management have been reported also in the Asian region, for instance, a nature reserve in the Tibet Autonomous Region of China and four protected areas of Nepal.[27]

Other efforts to manage resources across national borders include the transfrontier exchange of wildlife. According to an agreement between South Africa and Angola, for instance, South Africa has agreed to export a portion of its excess elephant population to the war-ravaged Angola. South Africa has 12,000 elephants and their numbers have reached saturation points in several parks.[28]

As will be explained below, this study supports the notion of managing transboundary resources transnationally. It prefers, though, the use of the term "transnational landscapes" instead of the term "transnational protected areas" for the purposes of emphasizing that the protection of biodiversity cannot be accomplished effectively without allowing for human use and habitation of many of the world's landscapes.

## 1.5. Restricted Access to Germplasm Resources

Today states attempt to control access to their germplasm resources by:

- setting so many restrictions that the access to germplasm within their borders is almost prohibitive;
- attempting to restrict the access to the resources located in the International Agricultural Research Centers;
- attempting to repatriate the resources located in international gene banks;

---

26 Arthur Westing, "A Transfrontier Reserve for Peace and Nature on the Korean Peninsula," in *Parks for Peace, id.* at 234.

27 Camille Richards, "Transboundary Collaboration in Biodiversity Conservation," *NepalNet*, available online at *http://www.panasia.org.sg/nepalnet/ecology/transbound.htm.*

28 Ed Stroddard, "South Africa to Export Excess Elephant Population to Angola," *Reuters News Service*, Sept. 4, 2000, available online at *http://www.reuters.com; see also* "First Elephants Airlifted from South Africa to Angola," *Afrol News,* Sept. 11, 2000, available online at *http://www.afrol.com.*

- attempting to prevent the assertion of intellectual property rights over resources initially found within their territory.

Restrictions of access to unknown germplasm and attempts to control the free exchange of seeds worldwide have jeopardized international gene bank development and have posed a threat to food security.

The only hope out of the bilateral restrictions on the free exchange of germplasm is offered by the Multilateral System established under the Treaty on Plant Genetic Resources for Food and Agriculture. This system, as articulated right now, allows for regulated free access to a small number of resources for food and agriculture. This study supports the expansion of regulated free access to all (*in situ* and *ex situ*) resources.[29]

## 2. PROPOSED INTERNATIONAL BIODIVERSITY MANAGEMENT

This study proposes that international policies could generate a fundamental shift in the way we think about biodiversity. International rules can call for biodiversity management instead of biodiversity preservation. And international rules can place human dignity at the core of biodiversity protection.

It is proposed here that the policy on biodiversity protection should be based on the admission that it is futile to attempt to preserve "pristine" biodiversity. Some biodiversity as we see it today will be converted to other uses. This is because of the causes of biodiversity conversion. As mentioned below,[30] these causes lie deep in the conditions of the developing world and are difficult to eradicate by quick remedies such as trade prohibitions and exclusive protected areas. This is especially so when the strict enforcement of these remedies is unacceptable from a human rights perspective.

As long as the majority of the people in the developing world remain poor and disenfranchised some of the biodiversity will be converted to other uses. Taking this conversion as a given, the best course of action

---

[29] *See infra* Section 2.5. *See also* Chapter 4.

[30] *See infra* Section 3.3.2.

policymakers can take is to establish standards and incentives to protect, at least, some of the evolution of the existing diversity. First order standards are human rights standards. Biodiversity must not be protected if such protection violates human rights norms as they have been articulated in the human rights instruments. Second, guidelines must be prescribed and incentives must be given, at the international and national level, for the consumptive uses of biodiversity resources to achieve as much as possible the sustainable management of those resources. Third, the guidelines should be implemented locally and people who live close to biodiversity-rich areas must be given the authority to decide how to best manage those areas. (For the proposed approach to biodiversity protection versus the current approach, *see* Table 2.)

## 2.1. Human Dignity and Human Rights as Threshold Standards

*Human Dignity and Human Solidarity*

Because the causes of biodiversity loss run deep in the economic conditions of the developing world, excluding people from officially designated protected areas will not achieve the goal of biodiversity protection. People will intrude the areas to plunder the resource and will be expelled in violation of their fundamental human rights. Therefore, it is necessary, when designating protected areas, that the interests and aspirations of people be granted central importance. Making human needs the center of biodiversity protection policies has been proposed so many times that it sounds trite. Many conservation programs claim today that they take into account human needs. For most of these programs, though, human needs are an afterthought in the service of biodiversity protection. It has happened rarely that biodiversity protection becomes the vehicle through which socials needs are met.

The human dignity standard proposed here and exemplified by human rights norms requires that the people of the developing world be viewed as the people whose needs are granted priority status in biodiversity protection. Human dignity demands that we look at other people, including the people of the developing world, the way we look at ourselves what Richard Rotry called "human solidarity." For most people, the

**Table 2: Protection of Biodiversity**

| | *Prevailing Approach* | *Proposed Approach* |
|---|---|---|
| *What* | Ecosystem *Preservation* | Ecosystem *Evolution* |
| *Why* | Because *Biodiversity* has value by Itself | Because biodiversity has value to the extent that it does not undermine *Human Rights Standards* and does relieve the *Poverty* in the Developing World |
| *How* | *National* Management/ *Strict* Enforcement | *Local/National/ International* Management/ *Self*-Enforcement |

phrase "one of us" means usually something smaller than the human race. Human solidarity is the ability to extend our sense of "we" to include people previously thought as "they."[31] Unfortunately, the people of the developing world are viewed often as either an obstacle to biodiversity protection or an instrument that could save biodiversity.[32]

It is proposed here that policies that do not pass the human dignity standard must not be applied for the protection of biodiversity. For

---

31 Richard Rotry, *Contingency, Irony and Solidarity* 191 (1989).

32 *See* David Takacs, *The Idea of Biodiversity* 212 (1996). (Dan Janzen, a conservation biologist, has stated: "[I]f you take a bunch of people out of any tropical region, and they don't have that level of biological literacy. . . . If you want those populations to manage their own natural resources . . . we've got to get them back to some basic understanding of what the natural history of the organism that they are managing. . . . And you just go into how appalling, *how appallingly biologically illiterate* these communities are. Well, if you go then and you educate those people—and I say give them back biocultural restoration, meaning give them biological literacy back—-that is a very economic argument, a very pragmatic one. You're [producing a population who are] happier, healthier, saner, *easier to manage*, and can manage their own affairs better. . . . [emphasis added].").

Some conservation biologists are even cruder. For instance Huge Iltis, a conservation biologist, derides his opponents as special interest groups whose environmental goals are "*colored by the need to help people* [emphasis added]." For Iltis, "if you put people first, you're lost right from the start. It's a slippery slope from which you can't get up once you start sliding." *Id.* at 182.

instance, policies that treat the people of the developing world as populations needing management and education to understand their own interests or as another type of resource do not meet the human dignity standard. Policies that render current generations poor and disenfranchised for the good of the future generations do not pass the human dignity standard. Policies that try to keep indigenous peoples as they are and do not respect the evolution of their culture do not meet this standard. Policies that demand the eviction of people from protected areas without their informed consent and without providing commensurate benefits, as defined by the people who are evicted, do not meet this standard.

The human dignity standard does not prescribe exactly what to do in order to protect biodiversity. It tells us, though, what not to do when biodiversity protection and human needs collide by granting unequivocal priority to the protection of human rights. In this sense, the human dignity standard is a negative standard that prescribes that development no matter its name—eco-development or industrial development—must not be achieved by creating more pain and suffering among the poor and the disenfranchised people of the developing world.

### *Human Dignity and Human Rights*

Human dignity must be at the core of biodiversity protection policies and the standards and incentives that support those policies. Human dignity has been the core of the human rights regime since the adoption of the first human rights instruments[33] but it is never referred to in the context of biodiversity protection. And yet it is in the context of biodiversity

---

[33] The first human rights instrument, the Universal Declaration of Human Rights, was adopted in 1948 after World War II. While the declaration is not a legally binding instrument, its provisions "either constitute general principles of law or represent elementary considerations of humanity." *See Basic Documents on Human Rights* 106 (Ian Brownlie ed., 1971).

According to Article 1 of the Universal Declaration of Human Rights:

> All human beings are born free and equal in dignity and rights. They are endowed with reason and conscience and should act towards one another in a spirit of brotherhood.

protection that many human rights norms are violated. This study proposes the development of an international regime in which human dignity and international biodiversity management are inextricably linked. Human dignity must become the theme of biodiversity protection and the core standard of biodiversity protection policies.

Human dignity as expressed in the human rights instruments is essential to achieve biodiversity protection with a humane face. Up until now international environmental policies juxtapose the terms "environment" and "development."[34] Governments of the developing world have argued that environmental protection cannot proceed unless the development and welfare of their population is secured. Since development has to do with human welfare, it is assumed that there is no reason to invoke human dignity as the cornerstone of biodiversity protection.

Development, though, is not synonymous with human rights. There is a difference between the counter-position of "environment" to "development" and the counter-position of "environment" to " human rights." Development can be viewed strictly as an increase in the Gross National Product (GNP). Human rights have to do with the prevention of torture, the right to property and the right to food.

Human rights are becoming even more instrumental when it is considered that biodiversity protection is becoming another vehicle for development. While it seems counterintuitive to see biodiversity protection as just another version of development, this is essentially what it is increasingly becoming. Today biodiversity protection involves intensive manipulation of ecosystems to produce a variety of goods from recreation to commercial production. Biodiversity protection is bound to become even more technocratic with the intensive application of bio-engineering and restoration. Since biodiversity protection is another expression of development, the balancing act that has to be performed is not between environmental values and development values. It is between two kinds of development. The welfare of humans in terms of the fulfillment of their basic, economic, political and social rights must be used to gauge the human rights implications of different types of development.

---

[34] The Rio Declaration on Environment and Development exemplifies the juxtaposition between environment and development. *See* Rio Declaration on Environment and Development, June 13, 1992, A/CONF.151/26 (Vol. 1).

Trusting the defense of the poor of the developing world to human rights standards will not always force governments to comply. Human rights norms are not absolute norms, they are subject to broad exceptions. The centerpiece of human rights protection—the International Covenant on Economic and Social Rights[35] and the International Covenant on Civil and Political Rights[36]—includes broad exceptions to the general human rights principles.[37] In addition, developing countries have often rebuffed western articulations that human rights are the inevitable outcome of the progress of civilization. Developing countries view human rights, instead, as the result of specific events—the American and French revolutions—that have shaped the cultural attitudes of the North. And Southern cultural attitudes do not have to mimic Northern cultural attitudes.[38]

---

35 International Covenant on Economic, Social and Cultural Rights, Dec. 16, 1966, General Assembly Resolution 2200A (XXI), *reprinted in Basic Documents on Human Rights* 199 (Ian Brownlie ed., 1971).

36 International Covenant on Civil and Political Rights, Dec. 16, 1966, General Assembly Resolution 2200A (XXI), *reprinted in Basic Documents on Human Rights* 211 (Ian Brownlie ed., 1971).

37 *See* art. 4 of the International Covenant on Economic, Social and Cultural Rights, *supra* note 35:

> The States Parties to the present Covenant recognize that . . . the State may subject such rights only to such limitations as are determined by law only in so far as this may be compatible with the nature of these rights and solely for the purpose of promoting the general welfare of the democratic society.

*See also* art. 4(1) of the International Covenant on Civil and Political Rights, *supra* note 36:

> In time of public emergency which threatens the life of the nation, the States Parties to the present Covenant may take measures derogating from their obligations under the present Covenant to the extent strictly required by the exigencies of the situation, provided that such measures are not inconsistent with their other obligations under international law and do not involve discrimination solely on the ground of race, colour, sex, language, religion or social origin.

38 African countries as they emerged from colonialism were the first to object to the universalistic nature of individual rights. African countries claimed that

Arguments aside, however, countries seem to agree on a quite large core of human rights. No country, for instance, could boldly claim that torture, famine, deprivation and degradation of human life are the inevitable prerequisite of development. Most countries, at least, attempt to pretend that they act in accordance with human rights norms.

The Vienna Declaration,[39] an outcome of the World Conference on Human Rights that took place in 1993, forged a consensus that human rights are universal, indivisible, interdependent and interrelated,[40] that human rights are a legitimate concern of the international community,[41] and that "human rights derive from the dignity and worth inherent in the human person."[42] The declaration even provides that "while development facilitates the enjoyment of all human rights, the lack of develop-

---

individual rights must be supplemented by peoples' rights and that the satisfaction of economic, social and cultural rights is the pre-requisite for the enjoyment of civil and political rights. African countries have included their claims in the African Charter on Human and Peoples Rights, which includes not only rights but also duties and provides for the right to development, the right to peace and the right to a satisfactory environment favorable to development. *See* African Charter on Human and Peoples' Rights (Banjul Charter), June 27, 1981, OAU Doc. CAB/LEG/67/3 rev.5, *reprinted in* 21 *I.L.M.* 58 (1982). For an analysis of the African Charter on Human Rights, *see* J. Oloka-Onyango, "Beyond Rhetoric: Reinvigorating the Struggle for Economic and Social Rights in Africa," *University of Minnesota Human Rights Library*, available online at *http://www1.umn.edu/humanrts/africa/Oloka-Onyango.html.*

The second challenge to individual rights has been launched by the economically invigorated Asian countries. The "Asian concept of human rights" was officially declared in the Bangkok Declaration on Human Rights, a preparatory document for the 1993 Vienna World Conference on Human Rights. Asian countries, like their African counterparts, emphasize that while some rights are universal, the western ideal of individual autonomy does not rime well with the Asian values that give priority to the community. *See* Bangkok Declaration on Human Rights, April 2, 1993, A/CONF. 157/ASRM/8.

39 Vienna Declaration and Programme of Action, World Conference on Human Rights, June 25, 1993, U.N. Doc. A/CONF.157/24 (Part I), at 20 (1993).

40 Art.1.

41 Art. 4.

42 Preamble.

ment may not be invoked to justify the abridgement of internationally recognized human rights."[43]

The overall acceptance of human rights norms and the number and prestige of non-governmental organizations (NGOs) that monitor the implementation of human rights litigate even more for the placement of biodiversity protection under a human rights umbrella. Governments have used environmental conservation or, put it differently, eco-development as a rationalization for engaging in egregious human rights violations. Notions dear to preservationists such as that of "pristine wilderness areas" have been used to expel people from their land and condemn them to more poverty. The anti-humanistic intonations of certain preservationist discourse are captured by governments and used to oppress populations under the pretext of strict enforcement of environmental law.

Today only a handful of human rights groups have paid attention to human rights violations perpetrated for the purposes of eco-development. This is because it seems paradoxical that environmental goals will be used to suppress human rights. Placing biodiversity protection under the human rights regime will put in place the checks and balances needed so that eco-development like all other types of development is not pursued at the expense of human dignity and human rights. (For a list of human rights relevant to biodiversity protection, *see* Table 3.)

## 2.2. Emphasis on Local Management Standards and Incentive Mechanisms

Human dignity, as expressed in the human rights instruments, is a necessary but not a sufficient standard for biodiversity protection. Additional management guidelines must be established for agriculture, forest clearance and all consumptive uses of diversity resources. And the goal of these guidelines must be the management and not the preservation of biodiversity resources. Cultivation and grazing must be performed in a fashion that allows for soil recovery. Logging also should be performed when certain guidelines and locally established standards are respected and enforced.

---

[43] Art. 10.

**Table 3: Human Rights Relevant for Biodiversity Management**

- Right to life, liberty and the security of person[1]
- Right not to be subjected to torture, or to cruel, inhuman and degrading punishment[2]
- Right not to be subjected to arbitrary arrest, detention and exile[3]
- Right for effective remedies before national tribunals[4]
- Right to self-determination[5]
- Right to an adequate standard of living, including adequate food, clothing and housing[6]

[1] Art. 3, Universal Declaration of Human Rights; arts. 6 and 9, International Covenant on Civil and Political Rights; art. 4, African Charter on Human and Peoples' Rights.

[2] Art. 5, Universal Declaration of Human Rights; art. 7, Covenant on Civil and Political Rights; art. 5, African Charter on Human and Peoples' Rights.

[3] Art. 7, Universal Declaration of Human Rights; art. 9, Covenant on Civil and Political Rights; art. 6, African Charter on Human and Peoples' Rights.

[4] Art. 8, Universal Declaration of Human Rights; arts. 9 and 14, Covenant on Civil and Political Rights; art. 7, African Charter on Human and Peoples' Rights.

[5] Art. 1, Covenant on Civil and Political Rights; art. 1, Covenant on Economic, Social and Cultural Rights; art. 20, African Charter on Human and Peoples' Rights.

[6] Art. 11, Covenant on Economic, Social and Cultural Rights; art. 22, African Charter on Human and Peoples' Rights.

In many cases management standards are difficult to establish and difficult to enforce. Often the standards are established by national and international institutions without taking into account local conditions and preferences.[44]

This study supports the development of standards for the protection of biodiversity. However, standards that prescribe the specific details of the management of a resource must be established locally, and, if this is possible, by the smallest cohesive unit that would have to apply the standards. National governments and international institutions could remain active in the designation of appropriate guidelines and recommendations for management. In addition, national and global institutions must provide incentives that would motivate people to endorse the guidelines and translate them into standards at the local level.

[44] *See supra* Section 1.2.

Many studies have proposed incentives, as opposed to top-down regulation/strict enforcement, as a means for the successful biodiversity management in the developing world. Incentives, though, are presented mostly in terms of the profits that can be extracted from specific non-consumptive activities such as bioprospecting, extractive reserves and ecotourism. It is only recently that the incentives proposed trumpet ownership of and responsibility for a resource as an effective incentive for the protection of the resource.[45] This study maintains that the most successful incentive measures are based on the control of the resource by the local people and emanate from secure land tenure.

As the benefits derived from the non-consumptive uses of biodiversity are falling behind expectations,[46] incentives must be designed to take into account the satisfaction of the immediate needs of people. Such incentives must incorporate the desire of people to assume control over their own affairs and develop a sort of growth that can be sustained both—in the short-term and in the long-term—and can bring significant wealth. To become supportive of biodiversity protection, people must acquire eventually control over the resources and be allowed to make decisions about the management of those resources under minimum guidelines prescribed internationally/nationally and applied locally.

International law cannot provide incentives based on resource control and secure land tenure. This type of incentives must be mandated nationally and take effect locally. However, international law can support the adoption of such incentives by removing the restrictions/prohibitions on the trade in wildlife species. The removal of barriers to international trade in wildlife could give governments the impetus they need to resuscitate and support local management systems.

Allowing people to get control over resources whose value is determined by free trade would do much more for poverty alleviation and biodiversity protection than other policies that rely on heavy-handed government intervention or other special interests' guidance. Secure land tenure, privatization and appropriation of wildlife supported by the free trade of wildlife resources could provide the incentives needed for the

---

45 *See* Chapter 2, Section 4.

46 *See* Chapter 2, Section 3.

creative use of biodiversity. Local resource control and free trade, under local management standards that incorporate human dignity values, could protect many of the species that are considered endangered today.

## 2.3. Free Trade in Wildlife as an Incentive for Local Management

Free trade in wildlife must be supported by international institutions as a means to encourage local wildlife management systems in developing countries. Freeing the trade in wildlife, though, is not as simple as it seems because of the vicious cycle in which this trade is trapped. Restrictions and prohibitions have perpetuated black markets that, in turn, have led to species loss. On one hand, lifting restrictions and prohibitions without supporting local grass root institutions willing to manage wildlife as a source of income will lead to even more mismanaged slaughtering. On the other hand, creating local management systems presupposes the lifting of restrictions so that there is real proof that there are benefits from sound wildlife management.

As will be seen below, some countries have experimented successfully with the creation of local wildlife management systems, and these countries have attempted to overhaul some the restrictions/prohibitions imposed by the CITES Convention.[47] These countries maintain that wildlife trade regulations as mandated by the CITES Convention are a rudimentary way to manage wildlife since the deep causes of wildlife conversion cannot really be resolved through trade measures.

This study proposes that, instead of trade prohibitions and restrictions, international biodiversity management must be based on the free trade in species and their products supported by the appropriate local management that includes human dignity and human rights values.

---

47 Critique submitted by Botswana, Malawi and Zimbabwe to the Secretariat and the Standing Committee of CITES in compliance with Notification No. 951 to the Parties of the "Study on How to Improve the Effectiveness of CITES" (1996), available online at *http://wildnetafrica.co.za/cites/info/iss_001_citescritique.html*.

## 2.4. Transnational Landscapes/International Conservancies

Even if biodiversity is squeezed into state boundaries, it is affected by global phenomena such as climate change that are beyond just a state's control. What happens in a diverse forest within one state can affect an adjacent forest in a neighboring state. Policies enacted in one state that are prohibitive of certain uses of biodiversity, simply shift the players to other states with more tolerant legislation. Efforts of states to ban access to resources within their jurisdiction can be frustrated easily if the state next to them allows access to the same resources. Overall management is less than optimal when the same ecosystem is managed by different states and institutions in accordance with different rules. Such management is bound to create duplication of effort and conflicting management policies.[48]

The matter of fact is that most of biodiversity is shared regionally or internationally[49] and that most of the forests of the developed and developing world often transcend national borders making strict concentration on national management futile. Regional ecosystem management then makes much more sense. The possibilities of wildlife transfers across national frontiers and of transboundary park development demonstrate that management should not stop at national borders. Transfrontier management projects, it is proposed here, should become the norm rather than the exception of biodiversity protection. In principle there is no reason for countries not to cooperate in the management of linked biodiversity areas. Such cooperation is taking place in Europe and in Latin America and it is currently attempted in Africa.[50]

---

48 Clare Shine, "Legal Mechanisms to Strengthen and Safeguard Transboundary Protected Areas," in *Parks for Peace, supra* note 24, at 37.

49 Joseph Henry Vogel, *Bioprospecting* 3 (final report commissioned by the Biodiversity Support Program on behalf of the Inter-American Commission on Biodiversity and Sustainable Development in preparation for the Summit of the Americas on Sustainable Development, Santa Cruz de la Sierra, Bolivia, December 6–8, 1996).

50 *See supra* Section 1.4.

The cooperative management of transnational areas presents many advantages.[51] This study favors transnational management for another reason. Transnational management can become a way to introduce more checks and balances and more transparency in the management of resources. Chances are that some of the countries involved in the co-management of a resource will not be as willing to oppress their populations and may exert a positive influence on others. Also human rights violations in transnational parks are likely to gain more publicity making transnational management a deterrent to the assaults on human dignity.

Despite these advantages, the joint management of common areas has not proceeded as quickly and smoothly as one would expect because of the obstacles involved. Such obstacles have to do with:

- nationalism, isolationism and different political ideologies among the states who share a resource;
- different laws with regard to the management of an area;
- religious differences, cultural differences and language barriers;
- different levels of political commitment creating a "weaker partner-dominant partner" situation;
- different degrees of discretion and authority granted to the agencies that manage the resource.[52]

Overall the management of transnational areas will only be nominal and will be paralyzed by indecision and inaction without the existence of common goals and leadership that would help surpass these obstacles.

While transnational management of transboundary resources is not easy, this study maintains it is worthwhile for countries to invest some of their resources in achieving such management. In addition to managing biodiversity more efficiently and effectively, transnational land-

---

51 Larry Hamilton, "Guidelines for Effective Transboundary Cooperation: Philosophy and Best Practices," in *Parks for Peace, supra* note 24, at 27 (the advantages of transfrontier management of protected areas include: reduction of the risk of biodiversity conversion in a well managed contiguous protected area; better implementation of management measures because of the joint efforts involved; better and cheaper marketing of the area because of the economies of scale involved (e.g., common maps, brochures, logos etc); improved staff morale).

52 *Id.*

scapes may help bring harmonization and peace in many of the troubled areas of the world.

To emphasize that transnational management must benefit the people who inhabit transboundary areas, this study proposes to replace the term "transnational protected areas" with the term "transnational landscapes." This is because of the ugly connotations associated with the term "protected area."[53] And because the term "transnational landscape" can help lock in the idea that human use/habitation and biodiversity protection are inextricably linked.

Under an optimistic scenario about the course of privatization of wildlife management,[54] transnational landscapes may eventually be transformed into *international conservancies*—a group of properties and wildlife resources managed communally by private landowners or communities across national borders. As long as this transition from public wildlife management to private wildlife management is completed with the full respect of international human rights, it is a welcome addition to the arsenal of means to improve the lives of people and protect biodiversity.

## 2.5. Regulated Free Access to Germplasm Resources and International Gene Bank Development

The development of international gene banks makes sense for three reasons:

- The collection and preservation of seeds from all over the world is by nature a transnational activity that involves many states and has to be undertaken by an institution that enjoys legitimacy in international circles;

---

[53] During a Parks for Peace Conference delegates from Southern Africa asked to replace the term "protected areas" with the term "trans-frontier conservation areas." The request came because of the "reputation which protected areas have had in the past in the region, as places from which local people are excluded and unable to gain any benefit from natural resources to which they have had traditional access." "Preface," in *Parks for Peace, supra* note 24, at v.

[54] *See* Chapter 2, Section 4.

- The collection and preservation of seeds is an expensive activity that can benefit from the economies of scale put together by many states;
- International gene banks are more institutionally stable than national gene banks since they depend on the collective will of states rather than the wishes and constraints of a single government.

Gene banks that contain seeds from all over the world are evidence that certain aspects of biodiversity protection can be managed best internationally. These seeds were preserved under a free access regime that allowed gene banks to collect them and preserve them in their collections. Without their collection from all over the world and their preservation in international, regional and national gene banks many of today's seeds would be extinct.

Gene bank development could in the future benefit from the economies of scale put together by national governments and international institutions to collect and preserve seeds. Seed collection and preservation are expensive and are bound to require even more resources as new technologies are put in place for the preservation and identification of resources.

Moreover, international gene banks, whose existence and development are based on the collective will of many governments, are more institutionally resilient than national gene banks that are constrained by the economic resources of just one country.

Despite the evidence that some aspects of biodiversity management make more sense on a regional or global basis, the movement today is more toward national management and control over biodiversity resources. As mentioned before, states—under the assumption that their biodiversity resources contain tremendous wealth—are zealous to preclude others from using those resources without at least paying first. While such strategies may prove profitable for known resources not yet preserved in national and international gene banks, they could backfire for resources of unknown use. Such resources will be wasted since the hefty entry fees will preclude experimentation with them. Companies are not willing to pay for unknown seeds lying in rainforests.[55] Attempts

---

[55] *See* Chapter 2, Section 3.1.

of states to prevent companies from asserting intellectual property rights over modified biodiversity resources may discourage companies to experiment with the resources.

As will be analyzed in Chapter 4, the prevalent nationalism and bilateralism that threaten the free exchange and transfer of seeds have been tempered recently by the adoption of a Multilateral System for the transfer of a restricted number of resources for food and agriculture. This is the first attempt to put in place an international regulatory system the purpose of which is to diminish the bureaucracy entailed in the myriad bilateral agreements that could be put in place for the transfer of plant genetic resources. Whether this system will become successful depends on the number and prestige of states that subscribe to it and the number of resources it covers. At this point the system covers only a small number of resources, and two major contributors to the negotiations of the treaty that established the system—the United States and Japan—refuse to subscribe to it because of concerns about the protection of intellectual property rights. The possibility of assertion of intellectual property rights over plant genetic resources was one of the most contentious issues during the negotiations of the Multilateral System since developing countries tried to establish rules that curtail the ability to assert intellectual property rights over plant genetic resources. Developing countries succeeded in establishing a mechanism that would help channel some of the gains from the commercialization of germplasm resources back to the farmers of the developing world who were the first to pinpoint to the right use of the resource.

A mechanism for the compensation of the people of the developing world for their contributions to biodiversity must help restore perceptions of equity and help legitimize a comprehensive system of regulated free access to resources. A compensation mechanism must help assuage many of the confrontations around the assertion of intellectual property rights over the modification of germplasm resources and could imbue a renewed sense of trust in the North-South relationships.

## 3. THE ASSUMPTIONS BEHIND THE POLICIES

The current policies on biodiversity protection are based on assumptions about what constitutes biodiversity and how to best manage it.

These assumptions provide a description of biodiversity as something *static* that needs to be preserved or conserved rather than as something *dynamic* that needs to be managed to achieve desirable social goals. Also most of the policies are based on the presumption that biodiversity needs to be protected because it has value above and beyond the servitude of human needs.

While these assumptions have been challenged by ecologists and anthropologists, who view biodiversity and humanity as inexorably linked, they still permeate many of the international biodiversity protection policies. Chapter 3 analyzes in detail the international policies that have been influenced by the static view of biodiversity protection.

## 3.1. Competing Definitions

### 3.1.1. Biodiversity as Ecosystem Preservation/ Biodiversity Loss as Extinction

Biodiversity is a term that has been developed by conservation biologists and is more or less equivalent to the terms "nature" and "wilderness" used in the past for the purposes of conservation. "Nature" is too generic a term to describe rich in diversity ecosystems and "wilderness" has been affiliated with the obsession of the white world to save natural areas. Biodiversity, on the other hand, is a fresh term that sounds scientific and could inspire public support. Conservation biologists have used the term to advocate the preservation of intact ecosystems and biological processes.[56]

When biodiversity is discussed the first image that comes to mind are the evergreen tropical forests. And there has been a crusade to protect these forests intact from modern development. Any land alteration that diminishes the primary forest is viewed as deforestation and biodiversity destruction. Many environmentalists believe that any forest removal will cause soil erosion, desertification and flooding and therefore they advocate the preservation of forests as they are.[57]

---

[56] *See* David Takacs, *The Idea of Biodiversity*, *supra* note 32, at 35.

[57] For an argument against this position, *see* L.S. Hamilton & A.J. Pearce, "Soil and Water Impact of Deforestation," in *Deforestation: Social Dynamics in*

The definition of biodiversity as something static that needs to be preserved intact is also obvious from the methods that have been used to "save biodiversity." As will be seen in Chapter 2, protected areas from which people are excluded are considered the ideal way to save biodiversity. Biodiversity loss has been attributed to human habitation and industrialism. As long as human habitation and industrialism persist biodiversity loss is inevitable. Any intervention, and particularly human intervention, is considered destruction of biodiversity. In short, the prevailing position is that biodiversity is something that needs to be preserved "as is" and must not be disturbed by humans.

Because biodiversity must be preserved as it is, any loss of biodiversity has been defined as extinction. The reported extinction rates are based on the species-area relationship. The species-area relationship[58] stands for the proposition that the number of species depends on the habitat available. As the habitat is shrinking, species become extinct. It has been projected that if the present rates of habitat destruction continue, the number of species will be reduced by at least one-half. This means that hundreds of thousands of species and, if insects are counted, millions of species are bound to become extinct.[59] In tropical forests extinctions are forecasted to be more severe than the extinctions in temperate regions, since the species in tropical regions are more localized. Some claim that the current biodiversity loss may be approaching the

---

*Watersheds and Mountain Ecosystems, supra* note 13, at 75, 83. *See also* L.S. Hamilton, "Forestry and Watershed Management," in *Deforestation, id.* at 99, 119.

[58] The species-area relationship is based on the theory of island biogeography. The theory of island biogeography is based on the principle that the larger the island, the larger the population size for any particular species and the smaller the chances that species will become extinct. This theory has been extrapolated to apply to other ecosystems. *See* D. Simberloff, "Do Species-Area Curves Predict Extinctions in Fragmented Forest?" in *Tropical Deforestation and Species Extinction* 75, 76 (T.C. Whitmore & J.A.Sayer eds., 1992). For a brief and comprehensive account of the island biogeography theory and its critics, *see* Graig L. Shafer, *Nature Reserves: Island Theory and Conservation in Practice* 11–33 (1990).

[59] For a summary of the different estimates of biodiversity loss, *see* Ariel E. Lugo, "Estimating Reductions in Diversity of Tropical Forest Species," in *Biodiversity* 58, 58–61 (E.O. Wilson ed., 1988).

massive losses triggered by natural disasters at the end of the Paleozoic and Mesozoic eras.[60]

### 3.1.2. Biodiversity as Ecosystem Evolution/Biodiversity Loss as Conversion

For many biologists, though, it is impossible to preserve intact ecosystems since extinction is a necessary part of the evolution.[61] Most ecosystems are not fragile to the point that any disturbance, human or natural, will cause ecosystem destruction and desertification.[62] Many ecosystems are resilient and thrive on "disturbance." Rain, floods, fire, winds and storms viewed through the human eye as disasters are part of ecosystem regulation.[63]

---

60 *See* E.O. Wilson, "The Current State of Biological Diversity," in *Biodiversity, id.* at 3; *See also* Norman Myers, "Tropical Forests and their Species: Going, Going . . . ?" in *Biodiversity, id.* at 28; Christoph Imboden, "Threatened Species: Birds as Indicators of Sustainability," in *Conserving Europe's Natural Heritage* 61, 62 (Graham Bennett ed., 1994); Robert M. May et al., "Assessing Extinction Rates," in *Extinction Rates* 1, 16 (John H. Lawton & Robert M. May eds., 1995); D. Simberloff, *supra* note 58; Beverly Peterson Stearns & Stephen C. Stearns, *Watching from the Edge of Extinction* (2000).

61 David M. Raup, "Diversity Crises in the Geological Past," in *Biodiversity, supra* note 59, at 51, 57 (species extinction is also a natural phenomenon. The average duration of species is less than 10 million years and the biological composition of the earth has changed many times. In fact extinction is a necessary part of the evolution. The fact that extinction is an essential component of the evolution should not give license to massively destroy ecosystems. However, it may shed perceptions that all ecosystem manipulation is equivalent to destruction and that biodiversity loss is necessarily irreversible).

62 Some ecologists debate whether we can actually talk about "ecosystems." According to one view, nature is comprised of a community of species that are organized together as a system. According to an opposing view, nature is comprised of collections of species whose habitats happen to coincide. *See* David M. Raup, *Extinction: Bad Genes or Bad Luck*? (1991).

63 There are many ecosystems that are dependent on disturbances such as the rainforest. These ecosystems cannot survive without those disturbances. *See* Richard J. Vogl, "The Ecological Factors that Produce Perturbation-Dependent Ecosystems," in *The Recovery Process in Damaged Ecosystems* 63 (John Cairns Jr. ed., 1980).

Humans have played a crucial role in enhancing species diversity.[64] It is hard to find today ecosystems that have not been affected by human actions. For instance, the Amazon is not the pristine rainforest it has been projected to be.[65] It has been slashed-and-burned for many centuries. When primary forests are removed secondary forests grow in their place. In many developed countries biodiversity resides in secondary forests.

Of course, not all human actions are favorable to diversity. Agricultural areas, for instance, are not as diverse as forested areas but are the most productive.[66] Humans have played an important role in diversifying or simplifying ecosystems according to their needs. A dynamic definition of diversity involves a view of diversity as ecosystem evolution. (For the dynamic definition of biodiversity as compared with the current definition, *see* figure 2.) And contributions to such evolution are both human and natural.

Accepting human intervention as part of ecosystem evolution gives a different spin to the allegations of biodiversity loss. First of all, even commentators that predict extensive biodiversity loss concede that the extent of biodiversity loss is dubious since the magnitude of biodiversity remains unknown.[67] Estimates of severe biodiversity loss consistently neglect mitigating factors such as the role of secondary forests as species refugia and the role of disturbance in maintaining species

---

[64] Darrell Addison Posey, "Interpreting and Applying the 'Reality' of Indigenous Concepts," in *Conservation of Neotropical Forests* 21, 28–29 (Kent H. Redford & Christine Padoch eds., 1992). *See also* William Balée, "People of the Fallow," in *Conservation of Neotropical Forests, id.* at 35.

[65] Jean-Louis Guillaumet, "Tropical Humid Forest Food Plants and Their Domestication," in *People and Food* 55 (*UNESCO Man & The Biosphere Series*, C.M. Hladik et al. ed., 1993); Doyle McKey et al., "Evolution and History in Tropical Forests in Relation to Food Availability," in *People and Food, id.* at 17.

[66] *See, e.g.*, Peter Herman May, *A Modern Tragedy of the Non-Commons* (dissertation thesis at Cornell University, 1986); G. Carlteton Ray, "Ecological Diversity in Coastal Zones and Oceans," in *Biodiversity, supra* note 59, at 36, 42.

[67] E.O. Wilson, "The Current State of Biological Diversity," in *Biodiversity, id.* at 3, 13.

**Figure 2: Definitions of Biodiversity**

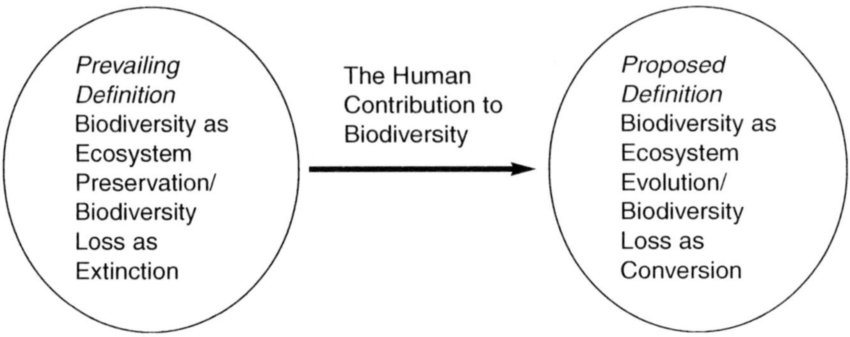


richness.[68] In addition, as mentioned above, human intervention is not synonymous with ecosystem degradation but with ecosystem homogenization. The decline in biodiversity is often a process of conversion from a variety of species to a smaller pool of species deemed worthy of propagation.[69] The history of agriculture and plantations involves exactly this process.

## 3.2. Competing Approaches to Managing Biodiversity

### 3.2.1. Avoid Management at All Costs

Ecosystem management is often criticized as an abnormal intrusion of humans into the workings of nature. In some environmental circles management is associated with consumptive uses: wildlife management for hunting, forest management for timber production, and range management for grazing. Under this view, ecosystem management has nothing to do with the preservation of "pristine ecosystems." And managing natural reserves is equivalent to treating nature like a zoo.[70]

---

68 Lugo, *supra* note 59, at 63–64.

69 Timothy Swanson, "The International Regulation of Biodiversity Decline," in *Biodiversity Loss: Economic and Ecological Issues* 225, 226–27 (Charles Perrings ed., 1995).

70 Frederic H. Wagner et al., *Wildlife Policies in the U.S. National Parks* 26

Many North American policies are based on the ideal that the natural environment can be preserved in a pristine state—free of human impacts. American parks were first established for recreational purposes but they increasingly evolved into areas to be secluded from humans. The goal of national park policy has been to maintain the parks " in the condition that prevailed when the area was first visited by the white man(,)" in a condition that represents a "vignette of primitive America."[71] This passage from Leopold is often cited to support the proposition that ideally parks must be natural areas isolated from human activities and that the essence of the wilderness is the absence of any sort of malevolent or benevolent human interaction.

The obsession to preserve pristine areas has detracted attention from areas in need of restoration. Restoration is ignored in international conservation policies because it cannot reproduce the "pristine" original ecosystem. Often a degraded ecosystem is viewed as a technical problem—not a conservation issue. While attention is focused on rich-biodiversity spots, ecologically jeopardized regions with degraded and unproductive soils are ignored even if restoring degraded areas can relieve pressure from areas deemed worthy of protection.

### 3.2.2. Management as a Necessity

Pristine areas, unaffected by humans, rarely exist making ecosystem management necessary in most protected areas. Active management is today pursued in many national parks in the United States, albeit ambivalently, and with the predisposition that it is not quite the right approach.[72]

In Europe, on the contrary, emphasis is placed on "landscapes" rather than "nature reserves." Landscapes cannot blossom without human intervention. Landscape management is based on the realization that the

---

(1995); *See also* Richard West Sellars, *Preserving Nature in National Parks: A History* (1999).

71 Wagner, *id.*

72 *Id.*

strict separation of the natural environment from the human factor is not possible.[73]

Protected areas are today patches of land surrounded by many uses. If they are not managed intensively they will deteriorate. Management may involve restoring severely depressed species; adding fertilizer to enhance degraded soil; or eliminating species that have grown too much jeopardizing the survival of other species.[74] The ultimate goal of management is not to freeze the ecosystem in its original state, but to support its evolution within the framework of larger societal goals. (For the proposed approach to ecosystem management versus the current approach, *see* Table 4.)

Active management of protected areas is often opposed because there is no perfect knowledge on how ecosystems function. If knowledge is incomplete management decisions will not always be successful. But lack of perfect knowledge should not lead to inaction. Some management decisions are easier to make, for instance, when because of hunting quotas a species has proliferated to such an extent that it is now becoming a threat to other species and the surrounding population. In this case resumption of hunting or reintroduction of a predator may be necessary.[75] Other management decisions will be more complex, for example, those pertaining to habitat manipulation and species

---

[73] Zev Naveh, "Biodiversity and Landscape Management," in *Biodiversity and Landscapes: A Paradox for Humanity* 187 (Ke Chung Kim & Robert D. Weaver eds., 1994).

[74] *See* Wagner, *supra* note 70, at 171–78. There is a significant amount of literature on wildlife management, *see* James H. Shaw, *Introduction to Wildlife Management* (1985); Graeme Caughley & Anthony R.E. Sinclair, *Wildlife Ecology and Management* (1994); *Living with Wildlife: Resource Management with Local Participation in Africa* (World Bank Technical Paper, Agnes Kiss ed., 1990); R. Sukumar, *The Asian Elephant: Ecology and Management* (1989); Michael E. Soulé, Bruce A. Wilcox & Claire Holtby, "Benign Neglect: A Model of Faunal Collapse in the Game Reserves of East Africa," in 15 *Biological Conservation* (No. 4) 259 (1979).

[75] Conservation groups have an aversion for culling animals even if culling is necessary to prevent degradation of nature reserves. Hunting is not viewed as an ideal way to control animal populations. *See Living with Wildlife*, *supra* note 74, at 23.

**Table 4: Biodiversity Management**

| *Prevalent Approach* | *Proposed Approach* |
|---|---|
| • Emphasis on Nature Reserves<br>• Minimization of Management of Protected Areas | • Emphasis on Landscapes<br>• Intensive Management including Restoration and Gene Banks |

reestablishment.[76] Transfers of plants and animals across borders should take place with caution, because the implications of the transfers to new ecosystems are not known.[77]

As protected areas become fewer and fewer, ecosystem management will evolve into restorative management. Today many ecosystems exist because of restorative efforts. While restoration can rarely bring back "original" ecosystems, it is instrumental in helping to avert soil erosion and in protecting the productivity of ecosystems. Edward Wilson has declared "the next century will . . . be the era of restoration in ecology."[78] And Soulé believes that "it is apparent that the emphasis on conservation biology will gradually shift from the protection of quasi-natural habitat fragments (. . .) to the opportunistic construction of artificially diverse landscapes."[79] Eventually the concept of "artificial nature" will become the future expected standard of biodiversity protection.[80]

Gene banks that have stored seeds for years are another example of biodiversity management.[81] The purpose of gene banks has been to collect and preserve seeds from all over the world. Gene banks are inter-

---

76 *See, e.g.*, H. Wagner et al., *Wildlife Policies in the U.S. National Parks* 178 (1995). *See also* James H. Shaw, *Introduction to Wildlife Management* (1985); Graeme Gaughley & Anthony R.E. Sinclair, *Wildlife Ecology and Management* (1994).

77 Soulé et al., *supra* note 74, at 270 (1979). *See* "An Elephantine Problem," *Economist*, May 30, 1996, at 75 (young elephants who have moved across national borders without the rest of the family become "rogue elephants" lacking "social graces" and having "serious attitude problems").

78 Takacs, *supra* note 56, at 205.

79 *Id.*

80 *See* Chapter 2, Section 5.

81 *See* Chapter 2, Section 6.

national, regional or national institutions that contain seeds mostly useful for agriculture. It is estimated that gene banks must contain most of the biodiversity useful for human purposes.[82] Gene banks have been instrumental in revitalizing the agricultural sector of countries after periods of war by re-introducing seeds that have disappeared due to war-related atrocities.

## 3.3. Competing Rationales for the Protection of Biodiversity

Different arguments have been proposed for the protection of biodiversity. Utilitarians claim that biodiversity must be protected because it brings spiritual renewal and economic profits. According to some ecologists, biodiversity is worth protecting because it has value by itself independent of whether it is useful for humans. This study proposes that biodiversity deserves to be protected only if it serves the goals of human dignity. (*See* Figure 3.)

### 3.3.1 Prevailing Rationale: Protecting Biodiversity for Biodiversity

*The Intrinsic Value of Biodiversity and Aesthetic Arguments*

The ecologists who support the protection of biodiversity for its intrinsic value argue that the interests of nature and ecosystems override the interests of humans. According to these ecologists, the current social paradigm has its roots in the Judeo-Christian tradition which views man as the sole purpose of creation. They propose a change: reconsidering life under an ecological-ethical perspective and re-inhabiting the land with hunting, gathering and gardening.[83]

---

82 *Id.*

83 This approach is often called Deep Ecology. Deep Ecology makes no efforts to disguise its basic tenet that all creation—human beings, animal, plants—must be put on an equal scale when deciding issues of preservation. *See, e.g.*, Lawrence E. Johnson, *A Morally Deep World: An Essay on Moral Significance and Environmental Ethics* (1993).

**Figure 3: Rationale for the Protection of Biodiversity**

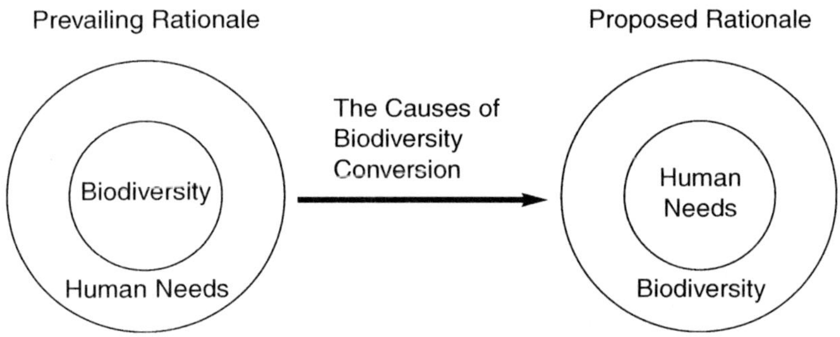


It is difficult to argue with this view—since it comes from a philosophical perspective on life that is against the progress in technology and industrialization as we experience it today. It is tempting to point out, though, that the interests of nature are unknown to people. Nature contains formidable sources of creation and destruction and what humans conceive as destruction is oftentimes the beginning of creation. Earthquakes, volcanoes, and the weather can alter ecosystems. Humans can do the same. From "nature's perspective" there is no reason to prefer the original ecosystem over what replaces it. Only by attaching values, a human preoccupation, it can be determined which ecosystem is preferable.[84]

Other ecologists aspiring to appeal to a wider audience support the protection of diversity on aesthetic values.[85] Who could argue after all against the preservation of a beautiful rainforest? As it turns out, many of the farmers of the developing world. Presenting aesthetic arguments as a rationale for biodiversity protection is a symptom of what Willams James has called "a certain blindness in human beings." James' illustration of this blindness was his personal experience during a trip to the Appalachian region where he saw the forest being decimated and being

---

84 For an eloquent rebuttal of the Deep Ecology Movement, *see* Luc Ferry, *Le Nouvel Ordre Ecologique* (1995). *See also* James J. Kay, "On the Nature of Ecological Integrity," in *Ecological Integrity and the Management of Ecosystems* (Stephen Woodley, James Kay & George Francis eds., 1990).

85 Takacs, *supra* note 56, at 217–68.

replaced by human constructs. James, after talking to the farmers, realized that "the clearing that was to [him] a mere ugly picture on the retina, was to them a symbol redolent with moral memories and sang a very paean of duty, struggle, and success."[86]

*Economic Arguments: The Benefits from the Non-Consumptive Uses of Biodiversity*

Since aesthetic arguments cannot easily convince farmers, economic arguments have been used: huge profits have been promised from the plants, insects and animals residing in the forests. According to the utilitarians, unlocking the information residing in biodiversity resources will help cure diseases and increase food supply. Forest plants could have medicinal properties. Pristine forests could attract ecotourists.

As will be analyzed in Chapter 2, the promised benefits from the non-consumptive uses have yet to materialize. Companies have not rushed into the forest to discover the latest life-saving seed. Most medicines and foods are prepared from well-known seeds and their varieties and not from unknown seeds lying in rainforests. Bioprospecting has not brought the wealth developing countries thought it would.[87] Extractivism has been sporadically successful, but it is unlikely that it would become the activity that will save the forests.[88] Ecotourism can be profitable in certain countries, for instance Africa, that have large and admirable mammals, but it will not necessarily be successful in all "pristine environments."[89] Most rainforests lack the large mammals that attract the tourists. Ecotourism also promotes the sort of "dependent development" that certain developing countries do not particularly favor.

Overall, most economic arguments presented to the South have been used as a pretext to preserve biodiversity while the underlying rationale

---

86 *See* William James, "On a Certain Blindness in Human Beings," in *Talks to Teachers on Psychology* 132,134 (Frederick Burkhardt & Fredson Bowers eds., 1983).

87 Chapter 2, Section 3.1.

88 Chapter 2, Section 3.2.

89 Chapter 2, Section 3.3.

remains—protection of biodiversity for its intrinsic value.[90] Propositions that non-consumptive uses of biodiversity are profitable to the point that they would exclude consumptive uses were not sustainable since their inception.

Other arguments that have been advanced use the terminology of finance to describe the value of biodiversity. Terms such as portfolio effect, option value and exploration value,[91] though, still sound distant to many ears. The poor of the developing world want to see the profits here and now because they experience the acute problems of deprivation. Developed countries believe that they have already collected the biodiversity useful for human purposes and have preserved it in their gene banks. Developed countries believe that future inventions will concentrate on the manipulation of these already discovered resources reducing the potential option value of unknown resources. Therefore, even the arguments about the future potential of biodiversity are unable to focus the international attention on biodiversity protection.

Because most economic arguments stressing the benefits from non-consumptive uses and potential future value of biodiversity have limited appeal to the diverse interests involved, the protection of biodiversity is anything but voluntary. As will be analyzed in Chapter 3, international environmental treaties do not always explicitly endorse the preservationist viewpoint—protection of biodiversity for biodiversity's sake. On the contrary, they often purport to balance environmental and development considerations and to take into account social and economic needs. Despite the rhetoric, though, environmental treaties are often applied in line with the strict protection of biodiver-

---

90 *See* Takacs, *supra* note 56, at 283.

91 The "portfolio effect" refers to the fact that the more diversified assets a portfolio includes, the less risky the portfolio becomes. The same is true with biodiversity, if biodiversity is high, the risk from sporadic extinctions will be lower. The option value refers to the fact that preserving resources is an option that may be "exercised" if certain resources become useful in the future. The exploration value refers to the fact that the exploration of new assets can lead to more discoveries of unknown characteristics. *See* Timothy Swanson, "The Appropriation of Evolution's Values," in *Intellectual Property Rights and Biodiversity Conservation* 141, 158–61 (Timothy M. Swanson ed., 1998).

sity to the exclusion of any use. This is because, from the perspective of governments, biodiversity protection is another sort of development that must be pursued for the national interest no matter the costs incurred in terms of violation of human rights. Enforcement of biodiversity protection laws comes, therefore, with the infliction of severe penalties and assaults on human dignity.

### 3.3.2. Proposed Rationale: Human Dignity at the Core of Biodiversity Protection

Human dignity is proposed here as the rationale and the basic standard for biodiversity protection. Most of the biodiversity resources are converted today because basic human needs—the satisfaction of which is essential to meet the human dignity standard—are neglected. People convert biodiversity-rich areas in their attempt to survive and "exercise" their right to food and shelter. This is obvious from the causes of biodiversity conversion. The causes of biodiversity conversion suggest that the protection of biodiversity, in order to become successful, must be designed to bring wealth to the communities that live around areas rich in biodiversity.

#### The Causes of Biodiversity Conversion

Biodiversity conversion in the developing world has been blamed on timber companies and on the slash-and-burn agriculturists who take over deforested areas and turn them into agricultural fields. However, more sophisticated studies have demonstrated that it is appropriate to distinguish between proximate threats and ultimate causes of biodiversity conversion. The proximate threats of biodiversity conversion include habitat destruction, deterioration and pollution while the ultimate causes of biodiversity conversion have to do with land tenure issues, population changes, cultural factors and national policy failures. (*See* Table 5.)[92] Overall, biodiversity conversion has been blamed on our "prevalent

---

[92] *See* Rowan Martin, "Biological Diversity: Diverging Views on its Status and Diverging Approaches to its Conservation," in *Earth Report 2000* 237 (Ronald Bailey ed., 2000).

approach to development"[93] which, at least at this point, is not forecasted to change.

*Logging as the Cause of Primary Forest Loss*

Logging may cause the destruction of many primary forests but it will not necessarily lead to deforestation and biodiversity reduction. After logging, if left undisturbed, primary forests are replaced by secondary forests that are also quite diverse. In general, the timber industry, while frequently responsible for the loss of primary forests, advocates forest conservation, in the form of secondary forests or plantations, and opposes the conversion of forests into agricultural fields.

The timber industry is a profitable industry in developing countries.[94] In Indonesia, for instance, exports of forest products account for 16 percent of the country's total export earnings only behind petroleum and gas in significance.[95] Attempting to halt primary forest removal, therefore, is futile especially when all the other non-consumptive uses of

93 *The Root Causes of Biodiversity Loss* 75 (Alexander Wood ed., 2000).

94 Tropical timber trade has been an easy source of revenue in many developing countries because of the tropical climate that makes possible shorter felling cycles and the low labor costs. *See* Jullian Evans, *Plantation Forestry in the Tropics* 19 (1992); Emmanuel D' Silva & S. Appanah, *Forestry Management for Sustainable Development* 7 (Economic Development Institute of the World Bank ed., 1993); William Chia, "Indonesia Firms Raise $850m from Bonds," *Business Times*, March 6, 1996, at 16.

95 "Jaya Holdings in Deal with Hasko Group," *Business Times*, April 16, 1996, at 1; Pratap Chatterjee, "Logging Threat Looms over Birds' Paradise," *Inter Press Service*, Feb. 6, 1996. Malaysia's timber sector is also extremely dynamic. *See* Stephen P. Loehnertz et al., "Hardwood Sawing Technology in Five Tropical Countries," 46(2) *Forest Products Journal* 51 (Feb. 1996). The timber sector of many Latin American countries is growing rapidly. The advantage of the climate has transformed Latin America from an importer of wood to an exporter of wood now accounting for 15 percent of the total world supply. *See* David Pilling, "Survey of World Forest Products," *Financial Times*, May 17, 1994, at III. Industrial timber products have been a significant source of revenue in Africa. However, many African countries have lost their market share to South-East Asia and developed countries.

**Table 5: The Causes of Biodiversity Conversion**

| Obvious Indicators | Deep Causes |
| --- | --- |
| • Logging | • Insecure Land Tenure |
| • Industrialization | • Poverty |
| • Pollution | • Population Pressures |

biodiversity do not bring nearly as much profit.[96] Countries view their forests as a renewable resource and will continue to clear forests as long as forest removal is profitable.

Prohibiting tropical timber trade[97] or switching to plantations will not save the primary forests. Prohibiting tropical timber trade will remove the economic value of forests and strengthen arguments to convert them into agricultural fields.[98] Timber plantations also render primary forests

---

96 *See* Chapter 2, Section 3.

97 For more details on the proposal to ban tropical timber trade, *see* Chapter 3, Section 1.

98 It is predicted that in the future most of the tropical wood will be consumed in the developing world and the South-to-North trade will be replaced with the South-to-South trade. Therefore a ban on imports from developing countries executed by the North will have little effect on consumption. Moreover a ban on tropical timber trade raises issues of fairness. *See* Edward Barbier & Michael Rauscher, "Policies to Control Tropical Deforestation: Trade Interventions versus Transfers," in *Biodiversity Loss: Economic and Ecological Issues* 260, 273–77 (Charles Perrings ed., 1995). *See also* E. Barbier et al., *Main Report to the International Timber Organization, Economic Linkages Between Trade in Tropical Timber and Sustainable Management of Forests* 30 (Final Report: ITTO Activity PCM XI/4, International Institute for Environment and Development ed., 1993). *See also* Joanne C. Burgess, "Biodiversity Loss Through Tropical Deforestation: The Role of Timber Production and Trade," in *Biodiversity Conservation* 237 (C.A. Parings et al. eds., 1995).

Wood from temperate forests is traded more extensively than tropical wood despite the fact that temperate forests present unique biodiversity. *See* Natalie Anger, "Redefining Diversity: Biologists Urge Look Beyond Rain Forests," *N. Y. Times*, Nov. 29, 1994, at C1 (some scientists argue that many of the species in rainforests are closely related. Therefore, rainforests may not be as diverse as it was indicated initially. Ecosystems such as deserts, temperate forests, and high altitude grasslands house less species but offer more genera, families or phyla).

useless and encourage their conversion to agricultural fields. Timber plantations are viewed by local people as a waste of agricultural land.[99]

*The Conversion of Forests into Agricultural Lands*

While logging is the primary cause of forest removal, it does not cause permanent deforestation. Permanent deforestation can be triggered when forests denuded by loggers are invaded by landless peasants who slash-and-burn and clear the forest to make room for agriculture and grazing. Of course slash-and-burn agriculture is not always the cause of biodiversity loss.[100] On the contrary, slash-and-burn agriculture many times enhances diversity and allows for forest regrowth. The problem is that today it is applied too intensively to allow for the recovery of forest ecosystems[101] though it is still considered more environmentally sound than mechanized farming and pasture development.[102]

---

99 *See* Elaine Morrison & Stephen M.J. Bass, "What About People?" in *Plantation Politics* 92 (Caroline Sargent & Stephen Bass eds., 1992); Philip Hirsch, "Forests, Forest Reserve and Forest Land in Thailand," 156 *The Geographical Journal* 166, 170 (1990); *See also* Gerald F. Murray, "The Wood Tree as a Peasant Cash-Crop: An Anthropological Study for the Domestication of Energy," in *Whose Trees? Proprietary Dimensions of Forestry* 215, 217 (Louise Fortmann & John W. Bruce eds., 1988).

100 Olive Mendelsohn & Upendra Baxi, *The Rights of Subordinated Peoples* 23 (1994).

101 Peter Dorner & William C. Thiesenhusen, *Land Tenure and Deforestation* 15 (United Nations Research Institute for Development ed., 1992). In Indonesia shifting cultivation covers an area of about 11 million hectares and is practiced by 1.2 million households or about six million people. *See* Theodore Panayotou & Somthawin Sungsuwan, *An Econometric Study of the Causes of Tropical Deforestation* 6 (Harvard Institute for International Development, Discussion Paper No. 284, March 1989). In Sumatra and Kalimatan, areas under extensive forest cover are intensively slashed and burned, *see* Edy Brotoisworo, "Indonesia Forest Resources and Management Policy," in *Technical Workshop to Explore Options for Global Forest Management* 254 (David Howlette & Caroline Sargent eds., 1991). In Sub-Saharan Africa forest areas are taken over by shifting cultivators at a rate of 0.6 hectares per year. *See* Narendra P. Sharma et al., *A Study for the Forest Sector in Sub-Saharan Africa* 29 (World Bank ed., 1994).

102 Hans P. Binswanger, "Brazilian Policies that Encourage the Deforestation in the Amazon," 19 *World Development* 821, 827 (1991).

The conversion of forests into agricultural lands has been blamed often on the short-sighted reluctance of peasants to make a long-term investment in forest preservation. Peasants, it is argued, are cultivating deforested land because they are unable to see the long-term and global benefits of forest preservation. Most cleared lands, according to this argument, are infertile and cannot sustain agricultural use for long periods of time. Therefore, the peasants who clear forests and insist on cultivating cleared land do so out of "ignorance or stupidity or both."[103]

Extensive research has demonstrated, though, that not all cleared land is infertile.[104] Moreover, productivity may not be in the minds of agriculturists when they cultivate and claim land. All over the world land has been used as a security or a speculative asset.[105] Untitled land has been used as a speculative asset in most countries that experience high rates of migration in forested areas. And many official migration pro-

---

[103] Michael H. Robinson, "Are There Alternatives to Destruction?" in *Biodiversity* 355 (E.O. Wilson ed., 1988).

[104] *See, e.g.*, Thomas T. Cochrane & Pedro A. Sanchez, "Land Resources, Soils and Their Management in the Amazon Region," in *Amazonia: Agriculture and Land Use Research* 137, 163 (Susanna B. Hecht ed., 1982, CIAT Series O3E-3(82)). In the Amazon not all soils are poor and subject to erosion after clearance. Erosion is unlikely to happen in the Amazon since secondary forests will take the place of primary forests. Some of the soil in the Amazon presents significant agricultural potential. *See* Herminio Maia Rocha, "General Evaluation of Development Policies and Research in the Brazilian Amazon," in *Amazonia, id.* at 33.

In Thailand most of the slash-and-burn practices affect the forests of *Dipterocarpus spp.* Such forests grow in areas suitable for agriculture. *See* Theodore Panayotou & Somthawin Sungsuwan, *supra* note 101, at 16. In Nepal the Tarai forest pursued for alternative uses is not part of the fragile areas of the Hills of Nepal. *See* Krishna Ghimire, *Forest or Farm?: The Politics of Poverty and Land Hunger in Nepal* 6–7 (1992).

Overall well-drained lands that support the best types of forests with good regeneration potential are the best for cultivation. *See* John Wyatt-Smith, "Problems and Prospects for Natural Management of Tropical Moist Forests," in *Natural Management of Tropical Moist Forests* 5, 19 (Francois Mergen & Jeffrey R. Vincent eds., 1987).

[105] *See* Chapter 2, notes 46 and 47.

grams,[106] that have acted as wealth distribution mechanism,[107] are responsible for the disappearance of forests all over the world. Overall, official transmigration programs, increasing populations and the reluctance of governments to deal with issues of perceived social inequity[108] make clearing the land, cultivating it and demanding rights to it an act motivated by the rational self-interest rather than an act spurred by irrational behavior.

*Remedies: Secure Land Tenure*

A plausible remedy for forest conversion may be secure land tenure. In most areas of the developing world most land resources used to be either common property resources or state resources. Common property regimes are rapidly disintegrating, though, under increasing populations

---

106 The colonization of the Amazon has been part of the official policy in Brazil. *See* "The Trans-Amazon Colonization Program," in *Sustainable Settlement in the Brazilian Amazon* 49 (Carl Jordan, Anna Luiza Ozorio de Almeida & João S. Campari eds., 1995). *See also* Gershon Feder, "The Economics of Land and Titling in Thailand," in *Economics of the Rural Organization* 259 (Karla Hoff, Avishay Braverman & Joseph E. Stiglitz eds., 1993).

Many transmigration programs are effective wealth distribution mechanisms. Most Amazonian migrants have benefited economically from settling in the Amazon. Most of the settlers plan to remain in the Amazon but only few plan to engage in agriculture. While the Amazonian settlers have low incomes they are still more affluent than half of the labor force in Brazil. *See* "The Trans-Amazon Colonization Project," in *Sustainable Settlement in the Brazilian Amazon, supra*, at 49.

The goal of the Indonesian transmigration program is to resettle households from the crowded areas of Java to the less populated areas and more ecologically diverse areas of Sumatra and Kalimatan. The transmigration program has alleviated poverty and has ensured a more equitable distribution of resources. *See* Yuli Ismartono, "Indonesia: Transmigration Eases Poverty but Threatens the Environment," *Inter Press Service*, Dec. 4, 1995.

107 See "The Trans-Amazon Colonization Project," in *Sustainable Development of the Brazilian Amazon, supra* note 106, at 49.

108 Population growth and the lack of alternative employment are often cited as the causes of biodiversity loss. *See* Panayotou, *supra* note 101, at 16, 21.

and the difficulty of local communities to exclude outsiders.[109] States also are often unable to monitor the resources that are under their jurisdiction. Today there is an attempt to replace most common property regimes and state property regimes with private property. Privatization, it is maintained, provides individuals and communities with incentives to upgrade and maintain the resource. The privatization of common

---

In many areas of the world land conflicts, due to what is perceived as the inequitable distribution of land, are still potent and often become violent. In Brazil, for instance, confrontations between the landowners and peasants are often violent. *See, e.g.*, Diana Jean Schemo, "Violence Growing in Battle Over Brazilian Land," *N.Y. Times*, April 21, 1996, Sec. 1, at 12, col. 1; Ana Maria Galano, "Land-Hungry in Brazil," Aug. 1998, available online at *http://www.unesco.org/courier/1998_08/uk/dicit/txt1.htm.*

Since countries, though, are reluctant to do anything that resembles redistribution of land, deforestation and the ensuing biodiversity conversion are bound to continue.

109 The inability to exclude outsiders transforms common property regimes to open access regimes. The resources of open access regimes are available to everybody without restriction. Common property regimes work well in traditional societies where communities are closed and there is a recognition and respect for local authorities. As long as the community is able to enforce its rights common property regimes can function smoothly.

But common property regimes disintegrate under increasing population pressures that make it more difficult to apportion the use of resources internally and exclude outsiders. This is especially true in forest areas invaded by a large number of migrants.

Common property regimes are viewed as regimes that benefit the poor. However, they have been subject to abuses when the community is internally divided and the regime favors the local elite rather than the majority of the population. Also occasionally the lack of individual property rights has benefited the rich landowners. For an analysis of the common property regimes and their pitfalls, *see* S. V. Ciriacy-Wantrup & Richard C. Bishop, " 'Common Property' as a Concept in Natural Resources Policy," 15 *Natural Resources Journal* 713 (1975); Garrett Hardin, "The Tragedy of the Commons," 162 *Science* 1243 (1968); *Proceedings of Conference on Common Property* (Office of International Affairs, National Research Council ed.,1986); Nancy Forster & David Stanfield, *Tenure Regimes and Forest Management* (Land Tenure Center, University of Wisconsin-Madison, March 1993); Pauline E. Peters, "Embedded Systems and Rooted Models," in *The Question of Commons* 171 (Bonnie J. McCay & James Acheson eds., 1987).

property resources, while not ideal,[110] has proceeded rapidly in many countries. As cash and perennial crops are introduced, population and migration increase and land becomes more scarce, property rights are more strongly asserted.[111] The privatization climate that is prevalent worldwide has precipitated attempts to introduce formal property titling in the developing word.[112]

Secure land tenure through privatization will not be a panacea for biodiversity conversion. As long as landless people and unexploited areas exist biodiversity conversion will continue. However, secure land tenure, which can be achieved through privatization, could help convince people to stay on their land and make the best of it, instead of constantly clearing land and engaging in speculative real estate transactions.

## People in Biodiversity Areas

Outsiders viewing the people in developing countries that live around biodiversity-rich areas usually place them in one of two categories:

---

110 Privatization of common property resources has proceeded rapidly in India but it has benefited the rich rather than the poor. *See* J.E.M. Arnold, *Common Property Management and Sustainable Development in India* 8–9 (1990). Privatization in Kenya has resulted in increasing disputes and litigation. *See* David Brokensha & Bernard Riley, "Forest Foraging, Fences and Fuel in a Marginal Area in Kenya," in *Whose Trees*? 102 (Louise Fortmann & John W. Bruce eds., 1988). Exclusionary private property regimes do not resolve the issue of what to do with the people who are left without property rights. Often poor people living on the fringes of common property regimes find themselves, on the onset of privatization, totally excluded from the use of the resource. *See* Nancy Forster & David Stanfield, *Tenure Regimes and Forest Management* (Land Tenure Center, University of Wisconsin-Madison, March 1993); Kathleen McNamara, "Key Policy Issues," in *Living with Trees: Policies and Forestry Management in Zimbabwe* 1, 4 (P.N. Bradley & K. McNamara eds., 1993).

111 *Land Tenure and Deforestation* (United Nations Research Institute for Development, Peter Dorner & William C. Thiesenhusen eds., 1992). However, areas of low productivity and areas difficult to divide will remain under common property regimes. *See* Bonnie J. McCay & James A Acheson, "Human Ecology of the Commons," in *The Question of Commons, supra* note 109 at 1, 17.

112 *See, e.g.*, "A Matter of Title," *Economist*, Dec. 9, 1995, at 47.

indigenous peoples[113] who must be allowed in nature reserves or squatters whose invasion of the reserved areas must be prohibited.[114] While

---

113 It is not easy to define "indigenous people." Most definitions of indigenous peoples consist of two elements: self-identification and external identification. For an individual to be called indigenous s/he must define herself/himself as indigenous and the group s/he belongs to must recognize her/him as a member. In Latin America, language, self-identification and geographic location have been used to determine who is indigenous. *See* George Psacharopoulos & Harry Antony Patrinos, *Indigenous Peoples and Poverty in Latin America* (World Bank ed., 1994). Canada and Australia have used similar criteria to identify indigenous peoples. *See* Guntram F.A. Werther, *Self-Determination in Western Democracies: Aboriginal Politics in Comparative Perspective* (1992). A treaty of the International Labor Organization (ILO) defines indigenous peoples as tribal peoples whose socioeconomic status is different from the rest of the nation and who are self-regulated or are regulated by special laws. The ILO convention provides also that self-identification should be a fundamental criterion in determining which groups are indigenous. *See* art. 1, Convention Concerning the Protection and Integration of Indigenous and Other Tribal and Semi-Tribal Populations in Independent Countries (Convention No. 169), June 7, 1989, 72 *I.L.O. Official Bull.* 59, *reprinted in* 28 *I.L.M.* 1382 (1989). A more progressive definition proposed by Martinez Cobo includes marginal or isolated populations who, while they have not suffered by conquest or colonization, still meet the criteria of distinct descent and culture and are isolated from the rest of the society. *See* Study of the Problem of Discrimination Against Indigenous Populations by José R. Martinez Cobo, Special Rapporteur of the Sub-Commission on Prevention of Discrimination and Protection of Minorities, E/CN.4/Sub.2/1986/ADD.4.

Overall it is difficult to find definitions that satisfy both governments and indigenous groups. Indigenous groups have claimed that self-identification should be the most decisive element in identifying who is indigenous and who is not. Other elements such as external identification based on distinctive culture and historic continuity should not be decisive since many people have evolved culturally and have been removed from their land.

114 It has been claimed that the emphasis placed on indigenous groups, and particularly the groups that live in the Amazon, has detracted attention from other groups that are mixed and constitute a large poor majority. The *caboclos* of the Amazon are often characterized as people of mixed Amerindian and Caucasian descent or simply as the "poor Portuguese speaking inhabitants" of the Amazon. The cultivation methods of *caboclos* have been praised by environmentalists and *caboclos* may soon become an updated symbol of environmentalism. *See* Kenneth I. Taylor, "Deforestation and Indians in the Brazilian Amazonia," in *Biodiversity*, *supra* note 59, at 138; Philip M. Fearnside, *The Human Carrying Capacity of the*

indigenous peoples are viewed as "species"[115] that must be protected other local groups are viewed as intruders who must be evicted. The strict distinction between indigenous people and other mixed populations, a result of our destructive obsession with racial purity, has been the cornerstone of many conservation policies. The matter of fact is, though, that secluded nature reserves will never survive when people are starving outside no matter whether they are called indigenous, squatters or peasants.

To be allowed in national parks, indigenous groups are instructed to use traditional methods such as bow and arrow—not firearms.[116] In the Cahuita Park of Costa Rica, it has been claimed that indigenous peoples must be excluded because their lifestyle has been altered by tourism and the cash economy.[117] Environmentalists support indigenous peoples when they confirm what is perceived as "traditional." Mixed people,

---

*Brazilian Rainforest* 18 n.5 (1986). For the recent migrants of the Amazon *caboclos* and Indians fall under the same category, the category of the poor. Both Indians and *caboclos* suffer from various diseases and they are undernourished. Today both Indians and *caboclos* are subject to the same pressures due to increased migration but they do not always co-exist harmoniously. Sometimes they form alliances such as the Alliance of Rainforest People, an association of indigenous groups and extractivists. *See* Stephen Nugent, *Amazonian Caboclo Society: An Essay on Invisibility and Peasant Economy* (1995); Allyn Maclean Stearman, "Neotropical Indigenous Hunters and Their Neighbors," in *The Conservation of Neotropical Forests* 108 (Kent H. Redford & Christine Padoch eds., 1992).

115 Many national and international development agencies, as well as environmental and human rights organizations, do not try to understand the political concerns of forest residents. Forest residents are seen as "passive victims," another "species" to be protected from extinction or helped by development. *See* Theodore MacDonald & Janet M. Chernela, *Politics, Development and the Indians* (unpublished manuscript, on file with the author).

116 *See* Patrick C. West & Steven R. Brechin, "National Parks, Protected Areas, and Resident Peoples," in *Resident Peoples and National Parks* 363 (Patrick C. West & Steven R. Brechin eds., 1991).

117 Kurt Kutay, "Cahuita National Park, Costa Rica," in *Resident Peoples, id.* at 114. *See also* Elizabeth Kemf, "Aluna: The Place Where the Mother was Born," in *The Law of the Mother* 131 (Elizabeth Kemf ed., 1993); Silvio Hernandez, "Panama: Indigenous People Ready to Fight for Land," *Inter Press Service*, Sept 29, 1995.

more or less integrated into the prevalent culture, do not qualify from a conservationist viewpoint to be called "indigenous."

This image of indigenous peoples as "ecologically noble savages"[118] living in isolated, self-sufficient communities and engaging happily in hunting and gathering has been discredited by anthropologists.[119] In real life indigenous peoples engage not only in hunting and gathering but also in agriculture. In addition, hunting and gathering in many societies are not performed for self-subsistence; they are targeted to commerce. In other words, while anthropologists in the past viewed hunting and gathering societies as self-reliant and communitarian,[120] a reflection of the paleolithic European past,[121] anthropologists today, not always unanimously,[122] have discovered mercantilism and capitalism in traditional societies. Hunters and gatherers of these societies are labeled "hot shot traders in the mercantile world for ivory and skin."[123]

---

118 The concept of "noble savage" was the product of European Enlightenment which viewed western civilization as corrupt and urged a return to nature. *See* Stephen Nugent, *Amazonian Caboclo Society* 235 (1995); *See also* Bernard W. Sheehan, *Seeds of Extinction* 90 (1974); Vine Deloria Jr., *The God is Red* (1973); Daniel J. Trainor, "Native American Mascots, Schools and the Title VI Hostile Environmental Analysis," 1995 *University of Illinois Law Review* 971; Kent Redford, "The Ecologically Noble Savage," 15 *Cultural Survival Quarterly* 46 (1990).

119 *See* Carl Hoffman, *The Punam: Hunters and Gatherers of Borneo* (1986). *See also* Serge Buhuchet, Doyle McKey & Igor de Garine, "Wild Yams Revisited: Is Independence from Agriculture Possible for Rain Forest Hunter-Gatherers?," 19 *Human Ecology* 213 (1991).

120 Not all indigenous societies are necessarily egalitarian, *see, e.g.*, Olga F. Linares, "Palm Oil Versus Palm Wine," in *People and Food*, *supra* note 65, at 595, 605.

121 "Western anthropology has created those societies labeled as forager as scientifically sanctioned survivors of an evolutionary past, that is, our *European* past . . . a past rooted in Euroamerican conceptions about the passage of events. Anthropology has thereby aided the overarching colonial process in appropriating these societies to our own histories to our own mythological use . . . these people have been left out without history." *See* Edwin N. Wilmsen, "Introduction," in *We Are Here: Politics of Aboriginal Land Tenure* 1,6 (Edwin N. Wilmsen ed., 1989).

122 Jacqueline S. Slowly & Richard B. Lee, "Foragers: Genuine or Spurious?," 31 *Current Anthropology* 109 (1990). *See also Politics and Histories in Band Societies* (Eleanor Leacock & Richard Lee eds., 1982).

123 Response of Schire to "Foragers: Genuine or Spurious?" *supra* note 122.

The conservationist ideal of indigenous peoples as "ecologically noble savages" has harmed indigenous groups[124] and distracted from their real problems, which often involve poverty and diminished health. The perception that indigenous groups live in communitarian societies with no concept of private property has allowed governments to expropriate their land.[125] Beliefs that indigenous cultures will disintegrate under the forces of modernity have legitimized paternalistic attitudes towards indigenous customs and beliefs.

Indigenous groups have claimed that equating them with nature is pejorative and violates their human rights. And for many indigenous groups self-determination involves the exploitation of natural resources including minerals, timber and game.[126] Many indigenous groups have collided with animal rights activists who consider unethical the killing of animals.[127]

Despite these ideological differences, many indigenous groups view the environmental movement, which enjoys prestige in international organizations and foundation circles, as a means to publicize their plight and attract favorable attention. In the beginning, this alliance between

---

124 Sheehan, *supra* note 118, at 102 ("[t]he subtle infiltration of noble savagism into the actual relationship between the white man and the native proved fatal to the survival of the Indian and seriously hampered the white man's perception of the consequences of his acts. . . . The Indian could not hope to equal the level of virtue attributed to him, because the primitivist formulations drew on a set of presuppositions wholly different from those within the reach of real men. Limited by the inertia of a time bound culture and threatened by cultural disintegration, the Indian could not but be pitied for his fate.").

125 For a discussion of ownership in traditional societies, *see Politics and History in Band Societies* 8 (Eleanor Leacock & Richard Lee eds., 1982); Robson Silitshena, "The Impact of Colonialism on Land Use in Central and South America," in *The Struggle for the Land* 146 (Paul A. Olson ed., 1990).

126 In North America and Canada many indigenous peoples' enterprises are based on the exploitation of natural resources. In the United States and Canada, indigenous peoples own logging, farming, ranching and fishing business. *See The Native North American Almanac* 921 (Duane Chapagne ed., 1994).

127 The livelihood of Canada's indigenous peoples is under constant threat due to the prohibitions in trading fur products.

the environmental movement and the indigenous peoples' movement[128] seemed promising only to disintegrate quickly because of the differing views held by conservationists and indigenous groups. Indigenous groups desire what all oppressed groups desire: power and control over their affairs.[129] The goal of the environmental movement, on the other hand, is the protection of the environment and humans are often a hindrance to that goal. A contentious issue between environmentalists and indigenous groups is land ownership. Indigenous groups desire unquestionable control over their lands. Environmentalists would rather prefer that nature reserves remain under government ownership and regulation. Behind the faith in government ownership lurks the belief that indigenous groups do not have the sophistication to handle complex issues of conservation and will be taken advantage of by ruthless corporations.[130]

---

128 The oppression of indigenous groups has sparked a strong indigenous movement. In the North most of the battles are fought in court or the negotiating table. In the South most battles are fought still on the ground. *See, e.g., Indigenous Peoples and Democracy in Latin America* (Donna Lee Van Cott ed., 1994).

129 There is a gap between the indigenous movement leadership and the groups it claims to represent. For instance, the Amazonian Indians have claimed often that the Confederation of Indigenous Nationalities of the Ecuadorian Amazon does not represent their interests. An agreement between the Confederation and a North American environmental organization, the Natural Resources Defense Council, was disapproved by the Amazonian Indians, *see* Joe Kane, "Letter from the Amazon," *New Yorker*, Sept. 27, 1993, at 54.

130 Janet M. Chernela, "Sustainability in Resource Rights and Conservation: The Case of an Awa Biosphere Reserve in Colombia and Ecuador," in *Indigenous Peoples and the Future of Amazonia: An Ecological Anthropology of an Endangered World* 245 (Leslie E. Sponsel ed., 1995).

A statement made by an Indian is characteristic of what indigenous groups are faced with:

> One of the biggest problems we've had to deal with in this political fight is just overcoming stereotypes and people's predisposition about how smart Indians are. We've had to spend an awful lot of time just convincing people that Indians are smart enough to deal with waste companies, and Indians are smart enough to regulate landfills and manage the environment. And that's the sort of thing you shouldn't have to prove in this day and age.
>
> Indian people have been told all their lives that they' re lazy, that they're ignorant, that they don't really want to do anything to improve themselves.

In the Amazon, where the players consist of a mixture of indigenous peoples and environmentalists, indigenous groups still form alliances with environmentalists against the big corporations. But the goals of indigenous groups differ from the goals of environmentalists. Environmentalists seek to prevent the development of the Amazon, while indigenous groups hope to use their resistance as a bargaining chip to obtain land concessions from the government. Indigenous groups in Latin America hope that one day they will be able to acquire land, mineral and timber rights as their counterparts in Canada and the United States have already done.

Many of the aspirations of indigenous peoples are reflected in the Draft Declaration on the Rights of Indigenous Peoples.[131] This declaration has yet to be adopted because countries are reluctant to endorse a document that may legitimize secessionist claims of the indigenous peoples living in their territory.[132]

Indigenous peoples have put forward also their recommendations for the revision of the policies of the World Bank. According to these recommendations,[133] which reverberate many of the provisions of the Draft Declaration:

---

> And here we are at Campo, we're trying to create jobs, we're trying to create income. We're trying to build houses, we're trying to build clinics, we're trying to get the kids go into college. And yet there are still people who want to keep us down.

Dan McGovern, "Experts from the Campo Indian Landfill War: Fight for Gold in California's Garbage," 14 *Stanford Environmental Law Journal* 375, 405 (1995).

131 Draft Declaration on the Rights of Indigenous Peoples, Aug. 26, 1994, E/CN.4/Sub.2/1994/2/Add.1.

132 *See, e.g.*, art. 31 of the Draft Declaration, *id.* "Indigenous peoples, as a specific form of exercising their right to self-determination, have the right to autonomy or self-government in matters relating to their internal and local affairs. . . ."

133 For an exhaustive list of these recommendations, *see* Thomas Griffiths & Marcus Colchester, *Indigenous Peoples, Forests and the World Bank: Policies and Practice* 8–10 (Draft Discussion Document, Workshop on Indigenous Peoples, Forests and the World Bank, May 9–10, 2000).

- the right of "self-identification" as indigenous must be recognized;
- indigenous peoples must not be involuntarily resettled. Resettlement can only take place with the full, prior, free and informed consent of affected indigenous communities. Resettlement cannot even be allowed in cases it "was demonstrated to be unavoidable;"
- the prior informed consent of indigenous peoples must be sought before their knowledge is disseminated and used by non-indigenous peoples;
- indigenous peoples must be consulted on their views on "appropriate compensation and mitigation measures" and must be involved in monitoring development projects.

It would be interesting to see how many of these recommendations the World Bank will adopt as policies and how many of these policies would be applied in practice.

# Chapter 2
# Evaluation of Biodiversity Protection Methods

This chapter examines the costs and benefits of biodiversity protection methods using human dignity as a benchmark. The discussion that follows demonstrates that biodiversity will not be protected if we just isolate an area, call it "park," and heavily guard it. What is needed instead is special attention to the unique conditions of the people involved. These conditions in most cases dictate that nature reserves that do not allow for consumptive uses and do not cater to the immediate needs of local people cannot be pursued successfully in the developing world.

## 1. APPLYING CONSERVATION: EMPIRICAL EVIDENCE

### 1.1. Strict Enforcement in Nature Reserves

Colonial governments were the first to impose environmental management accompanied by strict enforcement in areas that were previously free access. These areas were isolated, called "nature reserves," and removed from productive use.[1] Similar policies are still implemented by the regimes that followed colonialism when it is realized that the revenues generated by the consumptive uses of protected areas, such as safari hunting and tourism, are a good source of foreign exchange. Revenues from the consumptive uses of protected areas are also a good supplement to the revenues provided by agriculture, mining, and forestry. When nature reserves can pay for their preservation, enforcement is so relentless that some commentators have characterized it "coercive conservation."[2] Evidence of this type of coercive conservation is provided below.

---

1 *Producing Nature and Poverty in Africa: Continuity and Change* (Vigdis Broch-Due & Richard A. Shroeder eds., 2000).

2 Nancy Peluso, "Coercive Conservation: The Politics of State Resource Control," 3 *Global Environmental Change—Human and Policy Dimensions* 199 (1993).

In Botswana, strict enforcement is the norm in the conservation of nature reserves. For instance, Botswana's government has been involved for the last twenty years in violent confrontations with the Tyua people who live outside the Wankie National Park. The Tyua people have been arrested and tortured if found hunting in the restricted areas of the park. There have been instances where the personnel of the Wildlife Department shot and killed people found in these areas. The Department of Wildlife sees the Tyua as poachers who are armed and must be dealt with aggressively. According to some accounts, 96 people were killed in 1992 alone. As one Tyua woman put it: "Just because these people say they are helping preserve the environment does not mean that they should be able to violate our human rights."[3]

The American Anthropological Association (AAA) has reported other such incidents in Botswana. For instance in 1997, the government tried to resettle several people who live outside the game reserve of Central Kalahari. The resettlement took place under a climate of intimidation. Up to two-thirds of the residents of some communities, mostly males, have been arrested by game scouts and the police force. Since the males in the families tend to be the bread-winners some of the families are now living below the level of poverty. People claim that they have been tortured or have received inhumane and degrading punishment. There have been cases were people died because of the injuries inflicted by game scouts.[4]

Kenya is another example of a country that has tried to enforce the strict exclusion of local people from nature reserves. In 1989, in order to preserve the elephant, Kenya led efforts to ban the ivory trade. While the ban was initially successful because of the generous international assistance, it became ineffectual when the assistance dried up. In Kenya,

---

3 Robert K. Hitchcock, "Centralization, Resource Depletion and Coercive Conservation among the Tuya of the Northeastern Kalahari," 23 *Human Ecology* 169 (1995). *See also* Robert K. Hitchcock, "International Human Rights, the Environment and Indigenous Peoples," 4 *Colorado Journal of International Environmental Law and Policy* 1 (1994).

4 Report to the AAA Committee for Human Rights, *Human Rights, Development and the Peoples of Central Kalahari Game Reserve, Botswana* (Human Rights Briefing Documents, Sept. 1997).

75 percent of the wildlife still roams outside reserved areas destroying farms and ranches and is persistently killed by apprehensive and frustrated locals.[5]

Kenya's efforts to evict indigenous groups under the pretext of conservation have persisted until today. On March 23, 2000, the Nairobi High Court decided to evict the Ogiek from their lands in the Tinet Forests. According to the court, "the eviction is for the purpose of saving the whole Kenya from possible environmental disaster."[6] The Ogiek have argued that depriving them of access to the forest infringes upon their right to life and livelihood.[7]

Coercive conservation has been institutionalized globally by the policies of the World Bank and its affiliates. The eco-development project at the Nagarahole Park in India supported by the funds of the World Bank and the Global Environment Facility (GEF) took place by evicting 6,000 tribal people (58 tribal settlements) out of their traditional lands. While the World Bank labeled the displacement voluntary many people were simply forbidden from continuing their traditional activities within the forests. Eventually the villagers asked the Bank's Inspection Panel to review the project. The Inspection Panel upheld the peoples' complaints and found that the Bank staff did not implement the Bank's policies.[8]

In 1994, the World Bank awarded a US$20 million GEF grant to the Philippines for the purposes of preserving that country's biodiversity. As the project is about to be completed indigenous peoples claim that:

---

5 "Why We Ought to Hunt Big Animals," *The Economist*, April 20, 1996, at 76; "Kenya Seeks Way to Save Its Wildlife," *Chicago Tribune*, Mar. 15, 1996, at 19.

6 "Green Smokescreen for Eviction of Forest People," *Survival International Newsletter*, Spring 2000.

7 *Id.*

8 *See* Thomas Griffiths and Marcus Colchester, *Indigenous Peoples, Forests and the World Bank: Polices and Practice* 20 (Workshop on Indigenous Peoples, Forests and the World Bank, May 2000).

- They are frustrated and disillusioned with delays in receiving promised funding.
- It is unjust to prevent them from pursuing their traditional activities.
- The NGOs use them to get funding without making sure that indigenous families get benefits.
- The project is just another "protectionist" conservation project that refuses to deal with controversial issues of land rights and customary access to forest resources.[9]

The legislation that provides the foundation for the National Integrated Protected Area System in the Philippines buttresses the claims of indigenous peoples. The law's objective is to preserve the customary rights of peoples in protected areas. But the law also aims to put protected areas under study so that "experts" can decide "where, when and how much natural resources local communities can extract" weakening thus local management systems.[10]

The establishment of Bwindi and Mgahinga National Parks in Uganda in 1991 with the input of international funds including funds from the GEF has resulted in the eviction of Batwa people from their traditional lands. The evictions have destroyed the local economy which is forest based and have led to the severe impoverishment of Batwa. Today some Batwa are beggars while others are landless laborers. The Batwa see land redistribution as their only hope to some sort of independence. A trust fund has recently been created to deal with the issues of land distribution, compensation and forest access. But the administration of the fund has been met with resistance and implementation has been slow.[11]

The conflicts between preservation and the survival of local people are bound to persist in the future given the large number of people who live in protected areas. In Latin America, for instance, 86 percent of

---

9 *Id.* at 21.

10 Marcus Colchester, "Beyond 'Participation': Indigenous Peoples, Biological Diversity Conservation and Protected Area Management," 47(3) *Unasylva* 33 (1996).

11 Griffiths, *supra* note 8, at 24.

protected areas are inhabited.[12] In India 69 percent of the protected areas are inhabited.[13] According to the International Union for the Conservation of Nature, 70 percent of all protected areas worldwide are inhabited[14] and most of the inhabitants are indigenous peoples.

Coercive conservation is also expressed in the "war" that some developing countries have waged against poachers. Poachers, though, as analyzed below, are often peasants who are willing to risk their lives because of the wealth promised by poaching. In Kenya, for instance, an anti-poaching patrol killed four elephant poachers who defied orders to surrender.[15] In Malawi, wardens often punish the poachers immediately instead of handing them over to the police as the law requires. Captured poachers are allegedly maimed, electrocuted, raped, or brutally killed by the wardens in Malawi's Liwonde National Park.[16] In Swaziland, anyone convicted for poaching must spend five years in prison, and if they cannot replace the slain animal, they must spend seven years in prison. Swazi rangers have been armed with assault rifles and are allowed to shoot to kill to protect themselves. They have killed at least two poachers in the last ten years and shot and wounded several others. Swaziland's game rangers are immune from prosecution and have the right to search and arrest without a warrant. It has been reported that "conservationists across Africa and elsewhere have said Swaziland's no-nonsense approach is a model for other countries in the continent."[17] In China anti-poaching laws are enforced strictly. A Chinese court has jailed a peasant for twenty years for killing three pandas and stabbing and injuring a police officer while resisting arrest. In the past, killers of pandas faced the death penalty in China.[18] In 1984, the Zimbabwe Parks

---

12 Colchester, *supra* note 10.

13 *Id.*

14 *Id.*

15 "Kenyan Wildlife Guards Kill Elephant Poachers," *Reuters News Service,* Jan. 4, 2001, available online at *http://www.reuters.com.*

16 "Malawi Poachers Pay Dearly," *Panafrican News Agency*, Feb. 14, 2000.

17 Ed Stoddard, "Tough Swaziland Laws Deter Rhino Poachers," *Reuters News Service*, June 1, 2001, available online at *http://www.reuters.com.*

18 "China Jails Farmer for 20 Years for Killing Pandas," *Reuters News Service,* Nov. 26, 1998, available online at *http://www.reuters.com.*

Department set up Operation Stronghold to defend the rhino, a military operation that defends wildlife with shoot-to-kill policies. Wardens were equipped with automatic weapons, and poaching was punished with five years in prison. Despite these measures, Zimbabwe's black rhino population declined from 1,400 to 381 between 1981 and 1994.[19]

The unquestionable enforcement of wildlife laws in national parks has generated grass root political action in indigenous and local communities all over the world.[20]

## 1.2. Prohibiting/Restricting Trade in Endangered Species: Black Markets and Poachers

It was hoped that the CITES Convention, analyzed in detail in Chapter 3, with the prohibitions and restrictions it has enacted against the trade of endangered species, would be the instrument to help save the species. But the opposite has happened. Many of the species that the CITES Convention was supposed to "save" remain endangered and others are added to the list while countries still quibble over whether trade prohibitions/restrictions are the best way to save the species. For instance, in the case of ivory trade, Kenya, Western governments, and conservationist groups are in support of the CITES ban on ivory trade, while Zimbabwe, Namibia, Botswana, and South Africa propagate lifting the ban to help support their conservation programs.[21] The ivory politics

---

19 Marcela Rabi, "Black Rhinos, Horn and Trade," 7 *TED Case Studies,* Jan. 1997, available online at *http://www.american.edu/TED/class/all.htm.*

20 *See, e.g.*, Roderick P. Neumann, "Local Challenges to Global Agendas: Conservation, Economic Liberalization and the Pastoralists' Rights Movement in Tanzania," 27(4) *Antipode* 363 (1995).

21 Between 1979 and 1989, ivory poachers reduced the elephant population in Africa from 1.3 million to 625,000. Parties to the CITES Convention decided, therefore, to ban all trade in elephant products. However, Southern African states, whose elephant populations grew during the worst poaching years, always resented the ban. At the CITES meeting held in Harare in 1997, Botswana, Namibia, Zimbabwe, and South Africa lobbied to allow the trading of ivory under the system of permits mandated by Appendix II of the CITES Convention and succeeded in removing the ban. Now Kenya and India are pushing for a return to the ban claiming that their elephant populations are suffering because of the increase in poaching. *See* Simon

have reached the point that allegations are made that illegal poachers in Zimbabwe are supported by conservationists and Western governments who want to discredit Zimbabwe's local wildlife management efforts.[22]

The functioning of the CITES Convention is undermined by the existence of black markets in the species and products that are under CITES protection. Trade restrictions and prohibitions fuel the black market and make illegal poaching an attractive activity for many people in developing countries.

### *Black Markets*

The black market in the species proclaimed endangered by CITES is flourishing. The most notable examples include the trade in ivory and in rhino horn.

The prices paid for ivory increased from $2.25 per pound in 1960 to $68 per pound in 1988, indicating that ivory is now traded more like gold and silver—as a hedge against inflation.[23] In 1998, ivory was worth $250 per pound in Japan.[24] A great deal of the illegal trade in ivory occurs regionally within Africa. African ivory markets are supported by local authorities, affect international trade and constitute the reason for the serious poaching of elephants throughout Africa. Diplomats and personnel from the military and international organizations are heavily involved in illegally exporting raw and worked ivory.[25]

---

Robinson, "Dying for Ivory," *Time Europe*, April 17, 2000, available online at *http://www.time.com/time/europe/magazine/20010417/ivory.html*.

22 "Poachers Kill 84 Elephants in Zimbabwe Park," *Reuters News Service* [Online], Nov. 24, 1999, available at *http://www.reuters.com*.

23 Testimony of Dr. Teresa M. Telecky, Director of the Wildlife Trade Program the Humane Society of the United States on the H.R. 39, The African Elephant Conservation Reauthorization Act of 1997 before the Subcommittee on Fisheries, Conservation, Wildlife & Oceans, Mar. 13, 1997, available online at *http://www.house.gov/resources/105cong/fishery/mar13.97/telecky.htm*.

24 *See* Jaya Mathur, "Legal Ivory Trade and CITES," 8 *TED Case Studies,* June 1998, available online at *http://www.american.edu/TED/class/all.htm*.

25 Esmond Martin & Daniel Stiles, *The Ivory Markets of Africa* (2000).

In 1990, the average cost per kilogram of an African rhinohorn was $10,284 while for an Asian horn this figure was $21,354. In some Asian countries like Taiwan, the cost per kilogram has reached $60,000. The average value of each horn is $80,000.[26] Nepal's efforts to boost the country's rhino population are frustrated by illegal hunting. Since 1996 poachers have killed 26 rhinos for their horn, which fetches Rs 50,000 in the local market. One kilogram of rhinoceros horn can bring as much as Rs 1.5 million. The principal buyers of this powder, that is believed to be an aphrodisiac, are the wealthy in Hong-Kong, Japan, Taiwan, Thailand, and Singapore.[27]

The black market in endangered species products is supported by the same states who are supposed to enforce the CITES Convention. States have enacted reservations against certain prohibitions of the CITES while others have refused to sign and ratify the treaty because of their cultural traditions. For instance, although China became a member of CITES in 1981, it remains the world's largest importer of rhino horn and manufacturer of rhino products. China re-exports rhino horn and products to other eastern Asian countries.

### *Poachers*

It is claimed often that conservation will win if developing countries strictly punish the poachers who destroy the wildlife. The question is then: who are these poachers?

A poaching organization is organized as follows: the heads of the organization who are sometimes government officials; the dealers who manage the operations; and the people who actually engage in poaching. Most poaching operations are highly organized and well connected to politicians who are willing to look the other way for a price. The poverty of some developing countries makes it easy for dealers to

---

[26] Karen Sack, "CITES Rhino Horn Trade Ban," 2 *TED Case Studies*, Jan. 1993, available online at *http://www.american.edu/TED/class/all.htm.*

[27] "World's Remaining 2,500 Asian Rhinos Threatened by Poachers, Loss of Habitat Due to Logging and Expanding Farms," Dec. 24, 2000, available online at *http://www.eces.org/articles/static/97763760064192.shtml.*

find people willing to risk their lives to poach wildlife. These are the people whose human rights and dignity are violated by wildlife departments.[28]

Sometimes crime syndicates organized during war times and comprised of businessmen and warlords do not only commit atrocities against the people but also poach animals. Most often, though, poachers who operate on the ground are poor villagers who engage in poaching with the support of the local population. Usually poachers come from the communities that surround rich-in-wildlife areas and are often sheltered by those communities.[29] Whether a local community supports the poachers or the state depends on how alienated it feels from the state.[30] For instance, in Zimbabwe before the CAMPFIRE[31] program people were very supportive of the poachers who were viewed as heroes. From 1980 to 1982 the Mahenye people continued to hunt in the Gonarezhou National Park despite the government's prohibitions and were supportive of the ivory hunters. Local people reasoned as follows: if they had been excluded from the park because of tourism then it made sense to hunt animals to extinction. After the species had become extinct, the tourists would not come and they would be able to return to their land.[32] After the adoption of the CAMPFIRE, though, poaching lost its support and actually was opposed by many communities.[33]

---

28 "Poachers Killed Five Elephants in World Famous Corbett National Park," *Reuters News Service*, Feb. 19, 2001, available online at *http:// www.reuters. com*; "Clipping the Wings of Poachers in Zimbabwe," *Animal People*, Nov. 2000.

29 *See* Mahesh Rangarajan et al., *People, Parks and Wildlife* (2000).

30 Vasant K. Saberwal, *Reconciling the Needs of Man and Wildlife in India* (American Society of International Law-Wildlife Interest Group, Sept. 1999).

31 For the details of the CAMPFIRE program, *see infra* Section 4.1.

32 H.J. Goodwin, I.J. Kent, K.T. Parker & M.J. Walpole, *Tourism, Conservation & Sustainable Development: Volume IV, The South-East Lowveld, Zimbabwe* (April 1997) (unpublished manuscript, on file with the author).

33 *See infra* Section 4.1.

## 2. FROM NATURE RESERVES TO CO-MANAGEMENT

Nature reserves and parks involve protection of biodiversity in its natural environment. As mentioned above, the two approaches to nature reserves—the European and North American—differ from each other.

In Europe active management is adopted openly since most "conservation" areas are "landscapes" created by humans. Landscapes are a mosaic of " seminatural forests, woodlands, and grasslands, and agricultural fields, and plantations, interspersed with hedgerows, terraces, roads, and settlements."[34] In landscapes humans function in harmony with the "natural ecosystems." They are the shapers and initiators of many ecosystems. Multipurpose reforestation, afforestation, restoration and ecosystem manipulation may be used to a greater or lesser extent for landscape management.[35] In Europe the term "ecological network" is used much more extensively than the term "nature reserve" which emphasizes again a view of ecosystem management as management of interconnected areas rather than of secluded spots in the national geography.[36]

In the United States nature reserves are still perceived as areas to be isolated from humans. The 1964 United States Wilderness Act made official the notion of nature as wilderness isolated from human impacts. According to the Act, nature parks are areas "where man himself is a visitor who does not remain."[37] Most parks, though, when they were initially established, were inhabited by the Indians who eventually became the parks' unwelcome guests. The establishment of the first national park

---

34 Zev Naveh, "Biodiversity and Landscape Management," in *Biodiversity and Landscapes* 187, 188 (Ke Chung Kim & Robert D. Weaver eds., 1994).

35 *Id.* at 202–03.

36 The European Union has formally established an Ecological Network (EECONET). *See Protecting Nature: Regional Reviews of Protected Areas* 107 (J.A. McNeely et al. eds., 1994); *See also* Ivan Voloscuk, "EECONET and Forests," in *Conserving Europe's Natural Heritage: Towards a European Ecological Network* 103 (Graham Bennett ed., 1994).

37 *See* 16 U.S.C. § 1131, Section 2(c ): "A wilderness . . . is hereby recognized as an area where the earth and its community of life are untrammeled by man, where man himself is a visitor who does not remain."

in the United States uprooted the indigenous peoples living there. The establishment of Yellowstone National Park in 1872 was made possible by evicting the resident Shoshone Indians. The evictions led to violent conflicts between the Shoshone and the park authorities. Three hundred people were killed in clashes in 1877.[38]

Despite the wide-held notions that the United States National Parks are wild areas secluded from humans, management is used often to revamp "degraded reserves." Regulated human use is allowed also but it often conflicts with the purist desire to preserve the ecosystem intact.[39]

Developing countries have supported strict nature reserves enticed by the potential of economic windfall and encouraged by international organizations, and have used the reserves as an excuse to suppress their indigenous populations. But the strict nature reserve model is under attack in the developing world because of the large numbers of landless people.[40] Reserves that are inadequately monitored are constantly infiltrated by local people who view them as arbitrary violations of their natural rights to forests. Local people do not hesitate to destroy forests to demonstrate their anger against governments.[41]

Even under a modern approach to nature reserves that attempts to exclude humans only from core reserve areas,[42] local people remain

---

[38] Colchester, *supra* note 10. *See also* Marcus Colchester, "This Park Is No Longer Your Land," July 2001, available online at *http://www.unesco.org/courier/2001_07/uk/planet.htm*.

[39] *See* Frederic H. Wagner et al., *Wildlife Policies in the U.S. National Parks* (1995).

[40] *See, e.g.*, R.H.V. Bell, "Conservation with a Human Face: Conflict and Reconciliation in African Land Use Planning," in *Conservation in Africa* 79, 88, (D. Anderson & R. Grove eds., 1987).

[41] *See, e.g.*, Jack Westoby, *Introduction to World Forestry* 34 (1989).

[42] The modern approach to forest area management presupposes the involvement of local communities by providing incentives to maintain the reserve rather than destroy it for the quick economic benefit. The International Union for Conservation of Nature and Natural Resources (IUCN) in a revision of protected areas added a category of "managed resource protected areas," areas managed for the "sustainable use" of the ecosystem. *See Guidelines for Protected Area Management Categories* 23 (IUCN ed., 1994). For other attempts to classify pro-

dissatisfied. The biosphere reserves proposed by the United Nations Educational, Scientific and Cultural Organization (UNESCO) are often cited as an example of this modern approach. The biosphere reserves contain a core conservation area and buffer zones where different uses are permitted.[43] But the distinction between core areas and buffer zones is not followed in practice. Most biosphere reserves today consist of a patchwork of preexisting national parks with no separation between core areas and buffer zones.[44] Wild animals enter freely buffer zones destroying crops and property.[45] Core areas are often fertile and buffer zones are degraded generating demands to open core areas to use.

Even with these mixed-use reserves, local people remain unhappy for two reasons:

- They believe that they are viewed as the instrument or object of conservation rather than the decisionmakers that should dictate biodiversity protection priorities and needs.
- They see nature reserves as a way to deprive them from access to land. It is not important that the land may be infertile. In their eyes, land has always value since it can be used as a security or a speculative asset.[46] Untitled land has been used as a specula-

---

tected areas, *see Managing Global Genetic Resources* (National Academy of Sciences ed., 1991); *Technologies to Sustain Tropical Forest Resources* (United States Office of Technology Assessment ed., 1994); *Guidelines on Conservation of Biological Diversity in Tropical Production Forests* (International Tropical Timber Organization Policy Development Series No. 5 ed., 1993).

43 For a good description of a biosphere reserve, *see* "Conservation of Genetic Resources," in *Tropical Forest Management* 41–44 (FAO paper 107, ed., 1993).

44 *See* Craig L. Shafer, *Nature Reserves: Island Theory and Conservation Practice* 77 (1990).

45 *See generally* R. Sukumar, *The Asian Elephant: Ecology and Management* (1989).

46 The colonization of the Amazon has been part of the official policy in Brazil. In the 1970s when a severe draught ravaged the highly populated northeast region, the President of Brazil proposed a highway construction across the Amazon that would allow for the colonization of the area. *See* "The Trans-Amazon Colonization Project," in Carl Jordan et al., *Sustainable Development in the Brazilian Amazon* 58 (1995).

tive asset in Brazil during the official transmigration program to the Amazon and in other countries where populations migrate to forested areas.[47]

Local people still view conservation as another government ruse to deprive them of land. As mentioned before, the first legislative instruments to protect wildlife by excluding human use were adopted by colonial powers. In India, for example, the British controlled tightly tribal hunting and swidden agriculture. When they left, people engaged in rampant hunting.[48] Today many people living around forests feel the same hostility against the regulations imposed by the national government. The principle that nature reserves cannot exist without some allowance for human use is often iterated but it is superficially applied. As the population increases, human habitation and conservation become irreconcilable.

Some propose that allowing for the use of a nature reserve is not sufficient: co-management or participation by local people in decision-making must be established. Co-management, though, in many cases means multiplication of bureaucracy and does not meet the aspirations of people who want to own the land and manage it according to their wishes.[49] In 1982 the International Union for the Conservation of Nature (IUCN) passed a resolution that advocated joint management projects between local people and park authorities.[50] But according to a study

---

In Thailand also land, especially untitled land, has been used as a speculative asset. In Thailand, while it is difficult to obtain formal title, taxes still have to be paid on untitled land. *See* Philip Hirsch, "Forests, Forest Reserve and Forest Land in Thailand," 156 *The Geographical Journal* 166, 169 (1990).

47 For instance, in the Amazon region the resale value of land has little to do with its productivity. Land is more or less treated like gold bullion. Possessing gold bullion is more important for the security it generates rather than for its usefulness. *See* Philip Fearnside, *The Human Carrying Capacity of the Brazilian Rainforest* 29–30 (1986).

48 Richard P. Tucker, "Resident Peoples and Wildlife Reserves in India," in *Resident Peoples and National Parks* 40 (Patrick C. West & Steven R. Brechin eds., 1991).

49 *See* Ken M. East, "Joint Management of Canada's Northern National Parks," in *Resident Peoples and National Parks, id.* at 333.

50 Colchester, *supra* note 10.

committed subsequently by the same organization, participatory projects have pursued often objectives that have nothing to do with the wishes of people they are supposed to help.[51] The World Bank has recognized also that many of the efforts to include local people are rhetorical and that most "joint management projects" treat local people as passive entities.[52]

## 3. THE NON-CONSUMPTIVE USES OF BIODIVERSITY

### 3.1. Bioprospecting

Bioprospecting, expected to flourish under the national sovereignty regime over biodiversity resources put in place by the Biodiversity Convention, has not brought the desired monetary benefits. The national sovereignty over biodiversity resources has been widely respected by multinational corporations and research institutes. Corporations and research institutes have agreed to pay certain fees and royalties for access to seeds located in the forests of developing countries. The National Cancer Institute of the United States, the New York Botanical Garden and private corporations have paid fees or promised royalties as an exchange for access to biodiversity resources.[53]

An agreement between the INBio institute, a nonprofit organization created by the Costa Rica government, and Merck, a United States pharmaceutical company, was the first effort to establish processes and fees for access to biodiversity resources. Merck paid an initial $1.1 million fee and agreed to transfer technology, train scientists, and pay royalties in case an INBio extract produces a viable product. The agreement was

---

[51] *Id.*

[52] *Id.*

[53] The New York Botanical Garden has done so. However, the Missouri Botanic Garden finds it inappropriate to have to pay fees because it is a nonprofit institution. *See* Sarah A. Laird, "Contracts for Biodiversity Prospecting," in *Biodiversity Prospecting* 99, 113 (Walter V. Reid et al. ed., 1993). *See also* Edgar J. Asebey & Jill D. Kempenaar, "Biodiversity Prospecting: Fulfilling the Mandate of the Biodiversity Convention," 28 *Vanderbilt Journal of Transnational Law* 703, 721 (1995); Walter V. Reid, "A New Lease of Life," in *Biodiversity Prospecting, id* at 1, 5.

heralded as a victory for developing countries because it practically recognized that the acquisition and use of germplasm should be compensated. At the same time, though, it signaled that biodiversity resources are not as lucrative as they have been presented to be. INBio has to provide Merck with 2,000 product extracts within two years. Given that Merck laboratories need to process 5,000 samples per week to be effective, the amount provided by the INBio is too small to be significant and proves that Merck places little emphasis on resources collected from nature.[54] According to the experts at Merck, the effort put into screening "tropical samples is fragmented and not adequate for a significant chance of success."[55]

In other biodiversity agreements the royalties negotiated are too small—usually within the range of 1 to 2 percent—and only if the final product incorporates the plant extract, or if the final product is used for the same purposes the plant extract was used traditionally. In addition some of the royalty is usually paid back to the collaborating institution for its research costs.[56] Of all the investment opportunities forests provide, bioprospecting returns are the least predictable and the slowest to materialize. On the average, at least ten years elapse between finding a promising compound and developing a successful drug. Investors are deterred by the low market value of what is called "unprocessed biodiversity"—plants and animals of unknown use.[57] Markets for untested germplasm do not really exist.

Given the minimal profits and the limited number of companies[58] that may be interested in bioprospecting, it is questionable whether bio-

---

54 Asebey, *supra* note 53, at 725–728.

55 Georg Albers-Schonberg, "The Pharmaceutical Discovery Process," in *Intellectual Property Rights and Biodiversity Conservation* 67, 91 (Timothy M. Swanson ed., 1998).

56 Asebey, *supra* note 54, at 730–32.

57 Laura Tangley, "Rain Forests for Profit," *Reuters News Service*, Aug. 20, 1998, available online at *http://forests.org/archive/general/prandben/htm*.

58 Today not that many companies engage in drug production from natural substances. Shaman Pharmaceuticals, a company dedicated to the production of natural remedies has filed for Chapter 11 bankruptcy protection. *See* Brendan Doherty,

prospecting agreements are worth the administrative, legal, and monitoring costs that are necessary to negotiate them and enforce them. Even companies and research institutions that are genuinely interested in exploring natural resources often try to take advantage of the fact that the Biodiversity Convention does not apply retroactively, and thus it is not applicable to germplasm stored in gene banks before its entry into force. As mentioned before, botanical gardens and gene banks have collected seeds much before the existence of the Biodiversity Convention. The access to and experimentation with seeds of known use located in gene banks involves much less bureaucracy and is more promising.

## 3.2. Extractive Reserves

Extractivism—the gathering of forest products for commercial purposes—has been advocated as an alternative to agriculture and logging that benefits biodiversity protection. When extractivism is adopted as an alternative to consumptive uses one of the issues to be resolved is the ability of the extractive reserve to produce eventually on a massive scale and market the products extracted.[59] The ability to produce on a massive scale is essential if the demand for a product increases and competitors enter the marketplace.

Developing extractive enterprises can be daunting.[60] On one hand, immediate profits cannot be promised because extractive reserves need time to develop. On the other hand, if a reserve is successful excessive demand can make it obsolete: other marketers may produce the products of the reserve reducing its competitive advantage.

---

"Shaman Falls Victim to the Law of the Jungle," *San Francisco Business Times*, Jan. 19, 2001, available online at *http://www.sanfracisco.bcentral.com/sanfracisco/stories/2001/01/22/story7.html*.

59 Jason Clay, "Some General Principles and Strategies for Developing Markets in North America and Europe for Non-Timber Forest Products, in Non-Timber Products from Tropical Forests," 9 *Advances in Economic Botany* 101 (1992).

60 Alfredo Kingo Oyama Homma, *The Dynamics of Extraction in Amazonia*, *id.* at 23. *See also* Paul Vantomme, *Forest Extractivism in Amazon: Is It a Sustainable and Economically Viable Activity?* (First International Symposium on Environmental Studies on Tropical Rain Forests, Oct. 1990, Manous, Brazil).

In the eyes of local people extractivism is a low-status activity.[61] Agriculture generates more cash and is more stable economically than extractivism. Extractivism is rarely competitive with other land uses and rarely brings the economic profits that would entice people to abandon other land uses.

## 3.3. Ecotourism

Ecotourism is distinguished from mass tourism (and other consumptive uses) in that it does not adversely affect the natural environment. Ecotourism has been advanced in developing countries as a source of income, foreign exchange and as a stimulator of the local economy.[62]

Ecotourism, while trumpeted as a non-consumptive use of biodiversity, may eventually become another consumptive use. Ecotourism, for all its benefits, does not provide a constant revenue stream and in many instances is practiced in a way that it is nothing more than another consumptive use of biodiversity hardly distinguishable from mass tourism. Some governments are supportive of ecotourism but others are not supportive of it because ecotourism can become a mode of "dependent development." Tourism is not a stable source of revenue, and its success depends on a variety of factors outside the control of the host country. After some time, the enviable national park in a country may lose its appeal and areas in other countries could become ecotourism magnets. Changes in taste, fluctuations in the global economy, and wars can depress the local economy if that economy is heavily dependent on tourism.[63]

At the local level, ecotourism is supported if the land devoted to it is unfit for agriculture. If the land is fertile and can be used for cultivation

---

61 Niger C. Sizer, "Socio-Economic Aspects in the Jau National Park, Amazonia," in *People and Food* 789 (*UNESCO Man & the Biosphere Series*, C.M. Hladik et al. eds.,1993).

62 *Guidelines: Development of National Parks and Protected Areas for Tourism* (World Tourism Organization & United Nations Environment Program eds., 1992) [hereinafter WTO Guidelines]. *See also* Clem Tisdell, "Ecotourism, Economics, and the Environment," 34(4) *Journal of Travel Research* 11, Spring 1996.

63 *WTO Guidelines, id.* at 23.

or grazing ecotourism is rarely welcome by the locals. Local people resent abandoning their activities to become guides for tourists[64] especially when the profits from tourism go to outsiders who have the capability to build the infrastructure necessary for tourism.

Tourism can also denigrade local cultures when traditional activities become a tourist attraction. Many of the activities in national parks have been characterized as nothing more than enforced primitivism. People who live in national parks often perform human zoo functions for curious tourists. In the Kagga Kamma Game Park of South Africa tourists pay $7 to see a Bushman. And the Bushmen receive $1.5 for each tourist who pays to view them.[65]

For environmentalists, ecotourism often conflicts with conservation interests. Buildings to accommodate tourists, restaurants, souvenir stores and the waste generated by tourists are not the optimal formula for the "intact nature reserves" environmentalists revere.[66] And it is always tempting to open high demand areas to more tourists, resulting in the conversion of those areas.

In conclusion, ecotourism is not always environmentally benign and could disrupt the life of local people by forcing them out of their tradi-

---

[64] Michael Wells & Katrina Brandon, *People and Parks* 47 (World Bank, World Wildlife Fund & U.S. Agency for International Development eds., 1992).

[65] *See* Suzanne Daley, "Endangered Bushmen Find Refuge in a Game Park," *N.Y. Times*, Jan. 18, 1996, at A4, col.3; Eddie Koch, "Botswana-Human Rights: Sacrificed on the Altar of Tourism," *Inter Press Service*, April 4, 1996; Donald G. McNeel Jr., "Maputo Elephant Reserve Journal," *N.Y. Times*, Mar. 7, 1996, at A4, col. 3. *See also* Kunda Dixit, "Nepal-Culture: Winds of Change Sweep Sherpaland," *Inter Press Service*, Sept 21, 1995; Kalinga Seneviratne, "Australia: Tourism Gives Aborigines Opportunity for Self-Reliance," *Inter Press Service*, Dec. 8, 1995.

[66] A serious problem in the most visited mountain of the world, Everest, is rubbish. The government of Nepal has attempted to clean the mountain which is often called the "world's highest junkyard." Nepal's national parks are also under pressure because of the increased demand for timber to build lodges. *See* Gopal Sharma, "Glimbers to Take 1.5 Tonnes of Trash off Everest," *Reuters World Service*, May 2, 1996; Akhilesh Upadhyay, "Nepal-Energy: Small Hydro-Power Schemes May Save Himalayan Forests," *Inter Press Service*, Oct. 26, 1995; Birman Maharjan, "Asia Environment: Tourism is Damaging Nature, and Itself, *Inter Press Service*," Oct. 3, 1994. *See generally* Michael Frome, *Regreening the National Parks* (1991).

tional land.[67] While ecotourism does bring money to countries that have the sort of wildlife ecotourists admire, it will not bring money to all the countries with nature reserves unless they engage in extensive marketing of the resources and amenities they have to offer.

## 4. PRIVATIZATION OF WILDLIFE MANAGEMENT

### 4.1. Privatization as Community Empowerment: CAMPFIRE and CABNRM

To avoid the enforcement problems inherent in prohibiting access, some countries have enacted laws to privatize wildlife. Under the privatization laws, landowners or rural communities acquire the exclusive rights to manage wildlife within their territory.[68] But the ownership of the wildlife still remains with the state.[69]

The argument for privatization comes from the realization that the threat of extinction is remote for animals that are cared for by private owners, for instance, pets and farm animals. The same then must hold true for wild animals when they are privately owned.[70] According to this argument, the fact that big mammals straddle national frontiers and consume large amounts of food should not be an obstacle to privatization. Ranches and zoos (which keep animals in habitats varying from 100 to 700 acres) are examples of efforts to contain and manage wildlife. While it may be difficult to imagine the elephant or the rhino as farm animals, this is how they must be seen in order to survive. The products that can be obtained from the elephants and rhinos and their appeal to tourists can be used to bring wealth to local communities and can contribute to the long-term protection of the species from extinction.

---

67 "Call to Review Proclamation of Year of Eco-Tourism," *Afrol News*, April 17, 2001, available online at *http://www.afrol.com*.

68 Wildlife is state-owned or is *res nullious* (without formal owner). *See* Kay Muir-Leresche & Robert H. Nelson, *Private Property Rights to Wildlife: The Southern African Experiment* 1 (International Center for Economic Research, April 2000).

69 Not all privatization involves transfer of property rights, *see generally* Paul Starr, "The Meaning of Privatization," 6 *Yale Law and Policy Review* 6 (1988).

70 *See* Michael 't Sas-Rolfes, *Rhinos: Conservation, Economics and Trade-offs* (Institute of Economic Affairs, 1995).

*Zimbabwe's Experience: The CAMPFIRE Program*

Zimbabwe has granted rights to rural communities to exploit wildlife and retain the benefits. These rights were granted by the Parks and Wildlife Act as early as 1975. By enacting the Parks and Wildlife Act the state proceeded, for the first time after colonialism, to grant rights to local communities to manage wildlife within their territory for their own benefit.

These rights were not put to use, though, until the mid-1980s when the appropriate legal authorities were identified to administer wildlife management. Rural District Councils, an administrative division of the Zimbabwean state, have been awarded the legal status of Appropriate Authority for the management of wildlife resources.[71] The Rural District Councils are supposed to devolve all the direct benefits from the management of wildlife to the producer communities (Wards)—the communities directly incurring the costs of wildlife management.[72] Today sixteen District Councils have been developed and there are over a hundred Wards in all sixteen districts.[73]

The Communal Area Management Program for Indigenous Resources (CAMPFIRE), through the administrative structure of Rural District Councils, Villages and Wards, works more or less like a cooperative. All the adults in the community are shareholders in the cooperative and they

---

71 "Acts, Amendments and Appropriate Authorities: CAMPFIRE's Legal Framework," Fact Sheet, *Campfire 2001*, available online at *http://www.campfire-zimbabwe.org/facts_03. html*. (The 1975 Parks and Wildlife Act was amended in 1982 to extend the utilization of wildlife to communal lands. In 1989 the government and several NGOs started an effort to bring the management of wildlife to life through the CAMPFIRE (Communal Area Management Programme for Indigenous Resources) Project. Other legislation that strengthened local communities and passed the management of wildlife on to local communities includes the Communal Land Act that classifies and defines communal lands and the Rural District Councils Act of 1982).

72 T. Mavenke, V. Dzingirai & I. Bond, *Local Participation as an Instrument of Conservation and Development: the Case of CAMPFIRE in Zimbabwe* (Scandinavian Seminar College, African Perspectives on Policies and Practices Supporting Sustainable Development, 1999).

73 *Id.*

receive benefits from employment and dividends from tourism, ivory culling and meat marketing.

The privatization of wildlife management has not obliterated government involvement. The government still sets the overall goals of conservation, auctions the locally produced ivory and provides expertise in wildlife management. Sometimes, though, the government is too intrusive. For instance, communities do no have the final say in selecting the safari operator or setting the hunting quotas within their territory.[74]

Zimbabwe's effort to privatize wildlife resources stems from the realization that wildlife cannot be protected by a system of nature reserves because:

- Most of the country's resources are outside national parks, on communal lands and privately-owned ranches.
- Many wildlife areas are "island reserves" with the threat of serious genetic inbreeding among several species.
- Some species are found at higher than optimum densities in protected areas. In many Zimbabwean parks, for instance, elephants have created serious environmental degradation.[75]

The privatization of wildlife management in Zimbabwe, through the CAMPFIRE program,[76] has abated illegal hunting and other illegal uses of the wildlife. Local residents trained as game scouts work to prevent poaching and contribute to wildlife management. Revenues raised from wildlife projects are used to manage resources. Each village has a

---

74 *Id.*

75 "Living with Wildlife: How Campfire Communities Conserve their Natural Resources," Fact Sheet, *Campfire 2001*, available online at *http://www.campfire-zimbabwe.org/facts_04.html.*

76 CAMPFIRE is a collaborative organization responsible for coordinating its members' involvement. Its members include: the CAMPFIRE Association which represents the Rural District Councils and chairs the CAMPFIRE collaboration, the Department of Nationals Parks and Wildlife Management, the Ministry of Local Government, Rural and Urban Development, the Zimbabwe Trust, the Africa Resources Trust, the World Wide Fund For Nature. *See* "Who Runs Campfire?" Fact Sheet, *Campfire 2001*, available online at *http://www.campfire-zimbabwe.org/more_05.html.*

wildlife committee which deals with animal counting, anti-poaching, environmental education and conflicts between rural residents and "problem animals"—animals that destroy crops and livestock.

Privatization has done wonders for the protection of the elephants. In 1990 Zimbabwe's elephant population was less than 4,000. Today it is well over 64,000. And this is because local communities have stopped viewing the elephant as a nuisance and have started to appreciate it as a renewable resource. In some districts, such as Bulilima Mangwe, elephant harvesting is the only source of income. With a trophy fee up to $12,000 and a daily hunting fee of $1,000 one elephant can realize $33,000 over the course of an average 21-day hunt. Normally the safari operator retains a daily fee, while the local communities receive the full trophy fees plus negotiated fees for the rental of the hunting concession. Because of the wealth created, local communities have become more tolerant to wildlife. The number of elephants killed for damaging crops has dropped and some communities have set aside land for elephant reserves.[77] Principles and techniques for wildlife management have been adapted and applied to other natural resources such as woodlands, water and grass.

However, even the CAMPFIRE program as applied today is not problem-free. There are complaints that the people who are disadvantaged by wildlife measures—by ceasing hunting or altering their way of life—are not really compensated.[78] One of the reasons for the lack of compensation may have to do with the way the profits are distributed[79] and the fact that marginal communities are easy to bypass with impunity.

The distribution of profits has become an issue in many communities. Rural District Councils are in many cases reluctant to distribute the

---

[77] "Sharing the Land: People and Elephants in Rural Zimbabwe," Fact Sheet, *Campfire 2001*, available online at *http://www.campfire-zimbabwe.org/facts _07.html.*

[78] Elias Madzudzo, *Communal Tenure, Motivational Dynamics and Sustainable Wildlife Management in Zimbabwe* (Center of Applied Sciences, University of Zimbabwe, 1997).

[79] Profits are distributed among wards and are subsequently shared among villages but it is claimed that wards are not reflective of the social relationships. *Id.*

profits to the lower management unit[80] because they see the money as a means to remedy their own fiscal problems. It is also disturbing that some proceeds from wildlife management remain unallocated.[81] Moreover, as Wards and District Councils increase, the gross annual benefit per household decreases. For instance, in 1996 the gross annual benefit per household was $11 or less in 75 percent of the Wards.[82]

Also programs like CAMPFIRE are not immune from the problems that plague many developing countries such as that of corruption of government officials. In 1996, Zimbabwe's parliament concluded in a report that Zimbabwe's Department of National Parks "is riddled by corruption, infighting and jealousy."[83] Zimbabwe's Department of National Parks is one of the agencies sponsoring the CAMPFIRE program.

Despite these problems, the CAMPFIRE program is much more successful in terms of poverty alleviation and biodiversity protection than all the prior attempts to develop nature reserves from which human use is excluded. Actually both the CAMPFIRE program and CBNRM program reviewed below were conceived not only as programs geared toward wildlife management but also as programs aimed at rural development and good governance. The purpose of these programs is to develop local management systems by mobilizing participatory processes and accountable leaders and by instilling a belief in people that they are in charge of their destiny.[84]

### *Namibia's Experience: The CBNRM Program*

Namibia's Community-Based Natural Resources Management (CBNRM) Program was launched in the early 1990s when the newly created Ministry

---

80 Just over 53 percent of the revenue is allocated to sub-district units. Maveneke, *supra* note 72.

81 Ten percent of the proceeds remain unallocated. *Id.*

82 *Id.*

83 *See* Testimony of Dr. Teresa Telecky, *supra* note 23. *See also supra* note 76.

84 Brian T.B. Jones, "Community Management of Natural Resources in Namibia," (Scandinavian Seminar College's Africa Project, 1999), available online at *iied.org/pdf/dry_ip90english.pdf.*

of Wildlife Conservation and Tourism carried surveys to identify community perspectives on wildlife management.[85] Because Namibia does not have administrative state subdivisions as clearly delineated as those of Zimbabwe, the law provides that any group of people residing in communal land could decide to have that land declared a *conservancy* by the Ministry of Environment and Tourism.[86] To have a communal land be declared a conservancy, the community has to go through an application process in which it has to provide the government with assurances that it can manage the land effectively. This involves providing the government with its listed membership, constitution, designed boundaries, administrative and financial competence, sustainable management and utilization objectives, and proof for accountability and transparency.[87]

Conservancies have existed in Namibia since 1968 but the concept applied to private property. A conservancy was officially defined in 1991 as a group of farms in which neighboring landowners have pooled their resources for the purposes of conserving and utilizing wildlife on their combined properties. These farms, it was eventually decided, could be private or communal.[88]

The first communal area conservancy was officially established in 1997 and by mid-1999 four more conservancies were formed.

The experience gained by Zimbabwe's CAMPFIRE program has been useful in Namibia. For instance, CAMPFIRE officials have advised that management and authority in the conservancies must rest in the lowest possible unit and that it is preferable if communities keep 100 percent of the income they generate without having to share it with the government. It was suggested also that the cash must be paid to each head of household who, in turn, must return the portion of the income

---

85 *Id.*

86 M.W. Murphree & S.C. Metcalfe, *Conservancy Policy and the CAMPFIRE Programme in Zimbabwe* (Center for Applied Sciences, University of Zimbabwe, Mar. 1997).

87 *Id.*

88 *Id.*

agreed upon for community purposes. This way each member knows how much he gets and how much goes to the community.[89]

Some claim that the conservancy model presents many advantages that are lacking in CAMPFIRE. The pre-ordained administrative structure of CAMPFIRE sometimes thwarts cooperation between areas even when such cooperation makes sense. The conservancy approach presents then the opportunity to go beyond rigid administrative boundaries to establish "strategic management zones" mandated by ecological and financial considerations.[90]

Establishing conservancies, though, is not an easy process. Sometimes it takes years for neighboring communities to decide the boundaries of a conservancy. Deciding the boundaries of a conservancy is becoming a difficult task due to the population increase in Namibia that has transformed many communal lands into open access areas.[91]

In terms of financial rewards per household from involvement in the CBNRM program one thing is sure: the CBNRM program is not the final answer to the alleviation of poverty in communal lands. The money provided, though, through the program, is essential for households to which even a few hundred dollars more per year can make a significant difference.[92]

## 4.2. Privatization as Reduction of Government Overload: The Private Conservancies

Conservancies were developed in private land in Zimbabwe, Namibia and South Africa[93] much before the communal programs for the man-

---

89 Jones, *supra* note 84.

90 Murphree, *supra* note 86.

91 Jones, *supra* note 84.

92 *Id.*

93 In South Africa private conservation started in the 1900s. In Namibia conservancies existed since 1968. In Zimbabwe the process of creating conservancies started in the late 1980s well before the creation of the Rural District Councils. *See* Murphree, *supra* note 86.

agement of resources. While the conservancies in communal land work like cooperatives in which members receive dividends from a joint company, conservancies in private land resemble more communally managed property. Landowners still keep ownership of their land and control of the wildlife but have agreed to pool their properties and resources together to create large and well-managed areas for the appropriate management of the wildlife. Private conservancies are based on a contract among the landowners of a specific area to manage wildlife communally within that area. Non-governmental organizations have supported the development of private conservancies as a means of wildlife management where traditional state enforcement has failed. As mentioned before, cash-stripped states have enforced environmental laws strictly but not consistently since it requires a tremendous amount of resources to monitor large and treacherous areas of land.

Large private conservancies have been promoted in Namibia, South Africa and Zimbabwe as a means to manage wildlife privately but in conditions that do not resemble the zoo-like environment of smaller ranches. In Namibia twelve conservancies cover a land of 1.2 million hectares. In Zimbabwe, an increasing number of conservancies cover a land of more than 6,000 square kilometers. The Savé Conservancy in Zimbabwe covers an area of 340,000 hectares.[94] The transaction costs involved in negotiating private conservancies are as substantial as the transaction costs involved in negotiating communal conservancies. In some cases conservancies owe their existence to the efforts of NGOs who are seeking to find a home for the protection of an endangered species.[95]

This is the case in Zimbabwe where two NGOs—the UK-based Beit Trust and WWF-Zimbabwe—played crucial roles in supporting the development of private conservancies as a home for the about to become extinct black rhino population.[96] This happened at a time when the cat-

---

94 Kay Muir-Leresche & Robert H. Nelson, *Private Property Rights to Wildlife: The Southern African Experiment* 16 (International Center for Economic Research, April 2000).

95 *Id.*

96 Michael De Alessi, *Private Conservation and Black Rhinos in Zimbabwe: The Savé Valley and Bubiana Conservancies* (Institute of Economic Affairs, 2000), available online at *http://www.iea.org.uk*.

tle ranchers in Zimbabwe—who had suffered a damaging drought in the beginning of the 1990s—were willing to consider the alternative of wildlife management to cattle ranching.[97]

Wildlife management is granted to conservancies comprised of two or more landholders who sign an agreement to engage in the joint management of wildlife. Each conservancy also signs an agreement with the state. In the strict legal sense wildlife is still not owned by anyone (*res nullious*), but it could be said that the landowners who control and manage the wildlife have become the *de facto* owners of the wildlife. This is so with the exception of the rhino population who is still under state protection as specified in the agreements between the landowners and the state.[98]

The development of private conservancies has benefited the rhino population. Since the formation of the conservancies and their relocation in conservancy territory the black rhino numbers are growing in Zimbabwe showing that privatization can work where other wildlife protection methods fail.[99] Privatization should eventually benefit private landowners. According to a 1994 Price Waterhouse report, it was estimated that the return on capital from cattle could range from 1 to 3 percent while the return on capital from wildlife could be at 11 percent.[100]

However, such returns have yet to materialize. The reintroduction of the buffalo and other wildlife in the conservancies has triggered complaints about the risk of spreading disease beyond the conservancies in the communal areas that surround conservancy territory. To prevent the spread of disease, the conservancies had to erect a veterinary fence electrified at 5000v.[101] The creation of the fence put the conservancies under immediate financial pressure, since it required a significant amount of

---

97 *Id.*

98 *Id.*

99 *Id.*

100 *Id.*

101 H.J. Goodwin, I.J. Kent, K.T. Parker & M.J. Walpole, *Tourism Conservation & Sustainable Development: Volume IV, The South-East Lowveld, Zimbabwe* (April 1997, unpublished manuscript, available on file with the author).

capital and increased complaints from the surrounding communities. Even today the local communities feel that the private landowners have isolated themselves behind electrified fences that have prevented the people from accessing the resources.[102]

Issues of equity have marred private conservancies since their inception. In Namibia 6,000 largely white owners occupy 40 percent of the land. In Zimbabwe 4,500 white landowners occupy 35 percent of the land including the best farmland in a nation of 12 million people.[103] It is not surprising then that the majority of the people view the private conservancies as just another way to benefit the wealthy white landowners and serve the conservationists who have an interest in African wildlife. Zimbabwe's government has adopted an ambivalent attitude toward the conservancies—supporting them because of the promise of future returns including foreign exchange and simultaneously sabotaging them by threatening to adopt laws that would strip private landowners of their effective control over the land and resources.[104]

Overall, the ambivalence of the law about the ownership of the wildlife and demands for land redistribution have undermined investors' confidence in the conservancy concept. The absence of black entrepreneurs in the conservancies has politicized the issue even more.[105] This general climate of uncertainty is unlikely to help in the future development of private conservancies.

## 4.3. Privatization and the Wildlife Industry

The private management of wildlife resources through communal and commercial programs has contributed to the success of the wildlife industry in the Southern African countries. The wildlife industry—which includes ecotourism, mass tourism, safari hunting, sale of live game, meat and other products—is thriving in all three Southern African countries (Zimbabwe, Namibia, and South Africa). In South Africa, for

---

102 *Id.* at 115–16.

103 Muir-Leresche, *supra* note 94, at 20–21.

104 *Id.*

105 *See* Murphree, *supra* note 86.

instance, 5,000 foreign hunters spent about $22 million in 1997. The sale of live game for the purposes of restocking other ranches earned $809,262.[106] In Zimbabwe tourism is the most rapidly growing sector of the economy and the main source of foreign exchange. In 1998, the revenues from tourism amounted to 7 percent of the GNP and direct employment from tourism was 80,000 jobs (8 percent of the total employment). Private conservancies have created more jobs than cattle ranching. For instance, the Savé Conservancy in Zimbabwe employed 350 people in cattle ranching but it is now estimated that lodges within the conservancy will provide 1,200 tourism-related jobs.[107] In terms of the wildlife activities that are the most profitable, it is estimated that 90 percent of the revenues in the CAMPFIRE program come from leasing sport-hunting rights to commercial safari operators.[108] While the systematic collection of data is still incomplete, it is estimated that the wildlife industry is a growth industry with increasing demand and commodity prices. This is in sharp contrast with the beef industry that has been experiencing diminishing demand and prices over the last two decades. Overall, the wildlife industry is an industry in which developing countries have a comparative advantage. The further privatization of the industry and stimulus from local management programs accompanied with free trade in wildlife products will allow countries to fully benefit from this comparative advantage.

To take full advantage of the wealth created by the wildlife industry, commentators have proposed that innovative ways must be pursued to link the communal management of resources with the private conservancies. Trans-tenure conservancies, conservancies that involve commercial and communal farmers, have been proposed as an alternative to the separation of private landowners from communal farmers. The question now is how to get communal farmers to acquire equity in the conservancies since they do not have formal ownership of the land or formal ownership of the wildlife in the areas they occupy.[109]

---

106 Muir-Leresche, *supra* note 94, at 14–15.

107 Goodwin, *supra* note 101, at 114.

108 Maveneke, *supra* note 72.

109 Murphree, *supra* note 86 (the Savé Valley Conservancy has proposed a structure that would formally bind the Conservancy with its neighbors. Five Rural

## 4.4. Biodiversity for Wealth: The Successful Privatization of Wildlife Management

Overall, even programs that support the appropriation of resources by locals as a method of wildlife management and distribution of wealth will malfunction if the institutions of a country are corrupt and if the beneficiaries are not well identified. To become successful, privatization of wildlife management must meet certain conditions:

- The existence of resources that can be readily managed. Resources that can be segregated and divided among local inhabitants/units are easier to privatize.
- The existence of a community in the case of privatization of communal lands. Community management is not possible if the people involved do not constitute a community, are fractionally divided and the profits end up in the hands of the few wealthy.
- The existence and recognition of local institutions that are representative of the people who actually manage the resource.
- Secure land tenure.[110] Secure land tenure does not necessarily mean ownership. It means that people who manage the wildlife must have secure and long-term arrangements with regard to the land in which they manage the wildlife;
- The identification, participation, and compensation of marginal actors (e.g., minority communities) that may shoulder the costs of biodiversity protection.
- Respect for the human rights of all affected stakeholders.

Privatization, in other words, cannot happen in a vacuum. It must take into account the political circumstances of the country involved. Political

---

District Councils have decided to work with the Savé Conservancy in a Joint Working Committee. Several ways have been proposed to have local communities become investors in private conservancies, for instance:

(1) the government could grant wildlife to the conservancies as an equity investment on behalf of the communities;

(2) communal lands could be invested in the conservancies rendering local communities shareholders in the conservancy venture).

110 *See* Chapter 1, Section 3.3.2.

considerations are bound to decrease the efficiency of privatization[111] and delay its application but addressing them within the privatization program will contribute to the long-term viability of privatization. Moreover, it would defeat the purpose of a privatization program, as it is envisioned here, if privatization becomes a means to override human rights considerations. Privatization programs that enclose an area of the land while the rest of the population is starving outside could be as cruel as nature reserves and will be undermined eventually by the same populations that resent today's secluded protected areas. Privatization as exclusion is even worse than public nature reserves, since it is armed by the will of profit-motivated landowners which is bound to be more effective than that of the slow and often corrupt state bureaucracies.

## 5. RESTORATION AS A BIODIVERSITY PROTECTION METHOD

At first, restoration seems to be at odds with biodiversity protection. It seems that if ecosystems need to be restored we have lost the battle to protect them.

As development proceeds in a rapid pace, though, and many ecosystems are degraded to the point that they cease to be productive, restoration will become the most applied method of ecosystem management.[112] According to a conservative estimate, 758 million hectares exist in the tropics with potential for restoration.[113] Countries such as Nigeria, Rwanda, and Madagascar can expand their forests, if they desire to do so, through planting and regeneration.

The criterion for successful restoration must not depend on whether the reconstructed community resembles the original. But instead, on

---

111 *See* Paul Starr, "The Meaning of Privatization," 6 *Yale Law and Policy Review* 6 (1988).

112 John Cairns Jr., "Introduction," in *The Recovery Process in Damaged Ecosystems* 1 (John Cairns Jr. ed., 1980). *See also* William R. Jordan III, "Ecological Restoration," in *Biodiversity* 311 (E. O. Wilson ed., 1988).

113 Lawrence S. Hamilton, "Restoration of Degraded Tropical Forests," *in Environmental Restoration: Science and Strategies for Restoring the Earth* 113, 117 (John J. Berger ed., 1990).

whether the restored community is able to perpetuate itself; whether it can resist invasion; whether it can be as productive as the original.[114] Sometimes restoring ecosystems may involve letting nature take its course. In other cases it may involve more intensive management. The restorer is like a farmer. S/he uses all the technology available to speed up the restoration process to achieve what is socially desirable. In severely degraded ecosystems the primary goal may be prevention of erosion. In areas with abundant human habitation, it may be socially desirable to restore an easily manageable ecosystem rather than the original ecosystem. For example, in the case of a degraded agricultural land that was developed on a previously forested area, restoration may not involve the return to the forest but to the field's original productivity.[115]

Restoring viable ecosystems is not a simple process. Creating ecosystems cheaply and quickly involves an understanding of the factors that guarantee the reparation of the ecosystem.[116] The more these factors are understood, the less costly restoration will be.

Because restoration is rarely attempted for the recreation of the "original" ecosystem,[117] it is not viewed as a true conservation method. Ecologists refuse to see restoration as a subject worthy of their attention.[118] According to them, restoration has nothing to do with conser-

---

114 J. Ewel, "Restoration is the Ultimate Test of Ecological Theory," in *Restoration Ecology: A Synthetic Approach to Ecological Research* 31 (William R. Jordan III, Michael E. Gilpin & John D. Aber eds., 1987).

115 *See* William R. Jordan III et al., "Restoration Ecology: Ecological Restoration as a Technique for Basic Research," in *Restoration Ecology, id.* at 3.

116 A.D. Bradshaw, "Restoration Ecology: An Acid Test for Ecology," in *Restoration Ecology, id.* at 23.

117 While restoration can occasionally bring back "authentic and original" systems, this is often not practical because of the costs involved. Furthermore, from a social perspective, restoration faithful to the original landscape may not be desirable.

118 Restoration is often presented as a technical problem rather than as a conservation method. Engineers who engage in restoration refuse to see any use in the ecological approach and ecologists consider land reclamation a subject unworthy of their attention. *See* A.D. Bradshaw, "The Reclamation of Derelict Land and the Ecology of the Ecosystems," in *Restoration Ecology, supra* note 114, at 53.

vation since it is impossible to bring back the climax ecosystem after its destruction. Despite these objections, restoration is increasingly becoming the centerpiece of biodiversity protection. In many cases nature reserves exist because of extensive restoration efforts.

## 6. PROTECTING NATURE OUTSIDE NATURE: GENE BANKS

Gene banks were developed in the 1970s and 1980s to preserve biodiversity that would otherwise disappear. The first gene banks were developed in Europe[119] for the same reason that makes them now indispensable in developing countries—the scarcity of land. Farmers, applying modern agricultural techniques to feed a rising population, were quick to discard traditional varieties.[120] The diversity of traditional crops was in danger and needed to be preserved.[121]

The purpose of gene banks is to keep safe and in good condition the seeds of traditional landraces and other varieties so that they can be used for future breeding and genetic engineering. Gene banks concentrate on traditional and advanced agricultural varieties and their wild relatives

---

Ecology is generally viewed as a subject on the complexity of the ecosystems. Ecology is taught by introducing students to the holistic nature of ecosystems rather than by presenting how from simpler parts whole systems can be made. Restoration ecology involves exactly that: the inquiry of how parts fit into the whole. *See* John L. Harper, "The Heuristic Value of Ecological Restoration," in *Restoration Ecology, id.* at 35.

119 The earliest collection of crop plants was assembled by Philippe de Vilmorin at Verrieres near Paris in the mid-nineteenth century. Subsequently collections were established in England, Germany, Sweden, and Australia. These collections consisted mainly of landraces obtained by plant scientists from other countries. The first systematic collection was developed by Vavilov in Russia. *See* Ottto H. Frankel, Anthony H.D. Brown & Jeremy J. Burdon, *The Conservation of Plant Biodiversity* 98 (1995).

120 Miguel A. Alteri & Laura C. Merrick, "Agroecology and In Situ Conservation of Native Crop Diversity in the Developing World," in *Biodiversity* 361 (E.O. Wilson ed., 1988).

121 *See generally* Donald L. Plucknett et al., *Gene Banks and the World's Food* (1987).

that are either under-used or under the threat of extinction.[122] Gene banks have been instrumental in the preservation of food crops. When wars decimate indigenous germplasm, gene banks intervene to rehabilitate the farming sector of the war ravaged country. For instance, the International Agricultural Research Centers have provided assistance when seeds of a variety of sorghum called zera zera were destroyed in an attack on a gene bank in Ethiopia during a political upheaval. Similar assistance was provided to Nicaragua and Cambodia after periods of social disruption.[123]

Today a total of 1,308 gene banks have been established worldwide. Worldwide holdings of crop germplasm amount to 4.4 million accessions, but the number of unique samples is smaller due to duplication.[124] Germplasm collections have been established in 130 countries, and the most unique collections are located in the International Agricultural Research Centers.[125]

Usually, gene banks preserve seeds at low-temperatures, but they can preserve seeds also in the field or *in vitro*. DNA banks are an alternative to traditional gene banks. DNA banks can preserve DNA sequences and whole genomes for research.[126]

---

122 *Id.* at 17–18.

123 *See generally* Ramesh Jaura, "Rwanda-Agriculture: North, South Cooperate to Revive Farming," *Inter Press Service*, May 22, 1995; Fred Powledge, "The Food Supply's Safety Net," 45 (No. 4) *Bioscience* 235, April 1995; H. Carrison Wilkes, "Plant Genetic Resources Over Ten Thousands Years," in *Seeds and Sovereignty* 67, 86, (Jack R. Kloppenburg Jr. ed., 1988).

124 *See* Report on the State of World's Plant Genetic Resources, April 22–27, 1996, CGRFA-EX2/96/2 [hereinafter Report].

125 *Id.*

126 DNA banks present the following advantages: DNA sequences can be stored indefinitely without requiring regeneration. Stored DNA samples could be freely imported for research purposes since they are not subject to the quarantine regulations that apply to plants and seeds. But reliable documentation is crucial for the use of DNA samples. While plant collections can be used even if their characteristics have been recorded inaccurately, the use of DNA samples depends on reliable information. Also the use of the samples requires a greater degree of technical knowledge. In order to develop DNA banks scientists must know which character-

For gene banks to be useful, they must carry information on the germplasm they contain. Every germplasm must be accompanied by what is called passport data—which includes information on how the germplasm was obtained and the site of origin.[127] Germplasm must be checked periodically to verify whether it is still viable.[128] Further evaluation of the germplasm may be needed to identify the reactions to physical stresses, pathogens, and predators.[129] But the evaluation of germplasm accessions is not performed as consistently as it should.[130] Most collections lack precise information regarding the place of origin of the seeds they contain.[131] It is estimated that information is complete for only 1 percent of the germplasm contained in gene banks.[132] In addition gene banks are vulnerable to natural disasters and war. Gene banks may face shortage of electricity, since gene banks preserve collections at low temperature, a prolonged power shortage could destroy their collections.[133] Other problems include lack of storage space and computer failure.[134]

---

istics of the plant they wish to preserve. Overall DNA banks cannot assist in the regeneration of species and could not be used today for their revival. For this reason, while it is important to develop an international network of DNA repositories, DNA banks are not an alternative to traditional gene banks even if the latter are more expensive. *See* Frankel, *supra* note 119, at 110–11.

127 Material that arrives in poor condition must be multiplied before storage. Seeds to be stored must be of high quality and of maximum viability. *Id.* at 113.

128 But because of the high costs of regeneration, researchers must strike a balance between the risk of losing a viable seed and regeneration. *Id.* at 90–91.

129 *Id.* at 114.

130 Extensive evaluation of accessions does not exist and the information that exists is not readily available. *See* Report, *supra* note 124, at 9.

131 *See* Frankel, *supra* note 119, at 106.

132 Peter S. Ashton, "Conservation of Biological Diversity in Botanical Gardens," in *Biodiversity* 269, 275 (E.O. Wilson ed., 1988).

133 Plucknett, *supra* note 121, at 81.

134 Forty-six percent of accessions held in national collections need regeneration. *See* Commission on Plant Genetic Resources, Sixth Session, Item 8 of the Provisional Agenda, Survey of Existing Data on *Ex Situ* Collections of Plant Genetic Resources for Food and Agriculture, June 19–30, 1995, CPGR-6/95/8 Annex (CPGR-Ex1/94/5 Annex).

Even national programs in developed countries,[135] lack the financial security and ability to plan ahead due to budget uncertainties. In most countries gene bank policies are developed on an *ad-hoc* basis and lack coherence. The lack of training restrains also many national programs.

In order to insure against national gene bank failure, efforts have been made to internationalize gene bank management through the International Agricultural Research Centers. Also efforts have been made to insure against the destruction of collections. Most gene banks today, to be on the safe side, save a large number of seeds to the point of creating excessive overlap and sacrificing valuable space.[136] Some gene banks are building back-up cooling equipment and generators and some countries are experimenting with storing germplasm in naturally cold and dry locations.[137]

Gene banks have been instrumental in preserving food crops but not in preserving wild species. This is because the value of many wild species is not known and the techniques to maintain and regenerate wild

---

[135] It is not only collections in developing countries that face problems. In the United States the National Seed Storage Laboratory (NSSL) is renowned for its twelve-inch reinforced concrete walls, vault doors, security systems and it can withstand tornadoes, earthquakes, vandalism and terrorism. Expensive infrastructure, however, does not compensate for good organization. According to critics, the germplasm collection is poorly organized. Many accessions lack passport and characterization data. In addition, over 25 percent of the accessions are not available and this number is increasing. Some evaluation data do not exist due to the shortage of personnel. The collapse of communism in Eastern Europe has put the collections of those countries in serious trouble. *See* Powledge, *supra* note 123.

[136] The accessions of the Center for the Improvement of Maize and Wheat (CIMMYT) contain between 5,000 and 17,000 seeds. The International Rice Research Institute (IRRI) preserves between 5,000 and 8,000 seeds per accession. The obsession with the high number of seeds derives from the realization that gene banks, like all human institutions, are vulnerable. The danger that gene banks may be destroyed increases the value of duplicate collections held at different locations. These duplicate collections can serve as a back-up mechanism in the event of power failure, fire or other hazards and disasters. *See* Plucknett, *supra* note 121, at 81.

[137] *Id.* at 83.

species are not very advanced.[138] Botanic gardens are geared more toward the protection of wild species.

Approximately 1,500 botanical gardens exist today of which nearly 700 contain germplasm collections. Botanical gardens face problems that are similar to the problems faced by gene banks. Many botanical gardens do not have information on their collections and lack space and facilities.[139] They are hampered also by policy and staff changes.

As analyzed in Chapter 4, the seeds kept in gene banks are today the subject of controversy. Some developing countries seek to repatriate these seeds, attempt to control the transfer of these seeds, and to avert the assertion of intellectual property rights over the modification of the seeds. Such efforts and their repercussions on innovation and food security are explored in detail in Chapter 4.

## 7. COMPARING AND CHOOSING BIODIVERSITY PROTECTION METHODS

Three measures are used to compare the desirability of using nature reserves, landscapes, privatization, gene banks, and restoration for the purposes of international biodiversity management: respect for human dignity, the effect on the wealth of the local population, and biodiversity protection.

### *Human Dignity*

*Nature Reserves:* Nature reserve management scores low in terms of compliance with the standards dictated by human dignity and human rights. This is because nature reserves are often established under gross violations of human rights. Even recent efforts to involve locals in the management of nature reserves have not impressed the people who seek control over their own affairs.

---

[138] Report, *supra* note 124, at 56.

[139] J.E. Hernández Bermejo, *Information on Ex Situ Collections Maintained in Botanic Gardens* iv (Commission of Plant Genetic Resources for Food and Agriculture ed., 1996).

*Landscapes and Privatization of Wildlife:* Replacing nature reserves with landscapes and a genuine effort to include local people in their management through privatization and secure land tenure could contribute in changing perceptions that biodiversity protection is all about protecting wildlife with little regard about the people who are making a living out of it.

Privatization can cure many of the ills of conservation as practiced until today. Privatization, though, can succumb also to the opportunism of private or communal landowners who may attempt to exclude other legitimate landholders or who may accumulate the profits for the benefit of an elite minority rather than the disadvantaged majorities.

*Restoration:* Restorative efforts in nature reserves could provoke human rights concerns, especially if it is believed that the way to restore a degraded area is to prevent people from using it. Most frequently, though, restoration is performed in areas that are so degraded that are of little interest to conservationists and local populations.

*Gene Banks:* Gene banks can hardly impose any human rights threats. On the contrary, as analyzed below, gene banks can benefit the poor of the developing world especially after wars and natural disasters. International gene banks, however, have been the subject of controversy when the seeds they freely provide end up in the hands of multinational corporations. Multinational corporations, after modifying such seeds, often declare quite expansive intellectual property rights over them. The affirmation of intellectual property rights over modified germplasm has been called "biopiracy." Chapter 4 analyzes the issues of access to germplasm, intellectual property rights and mechanisms for the compensation of indigenous peoples and farmers.

### *The Wealth Effect*

*Nature Reserves:* Nature reserves have not brought the promised wealth to local communities. The propagated non-consumptive uses of nature reserves, such as extractivism and bioprospecting, are not as lucrative as initially promised and have disappointed local communities. The wealth brought by these activities is not even comparable to the wealth brought by traditional consumptive uses such as agriculture, grazing and tourism. For instance, the total value of INBio's activities in Costa Rica is $1 million—a minimal amount compared to the revenues generated by forestry and tourism. Costa Rica's forestry industry generated $28 million while its tourism generated $421 million.[140]

*Landscapes and Privatization of Wildlife Management:* The Zimbabwean efforts to privatize wildlife seem to be the most promising in terms of increasing the wealth of the local population. Privatization of wildlife in communal or private lands can bring wealth as landowners and communities become involved in the wildlife trade and the tourism industry. How much privatization accomplishes in terms of benefits to local populations depends on how it is applied. Unless privatization is performed in a manner that addresses social equity issues and community empowerment, it could become the subject of severe criticism and eventually fail. All privatization programs, since they are envisioned as a remedy to the ills caused by nature reserves, must be performed with full respect of human rights.

*Restoration/Gene Banks:* Restoring degraded ecosystems can bring wealth to local communities. Many restoration efforts have already been successful in re-establishing productive ecosystems. And many gene banks have been able to preserve seeds that have been used to produce enhanced varieties and to rejuvenate the agricultural sector of developing countries after periods of war and natural disasters.

### *Ability to Protect Biodiversity*

*Nature Reserves:* As mentioned before, many natural ecosystems in the tropics are "disturbance-dependent" and thrive under what are perceived by humans to be catastrophes. Sometimes, though, human impacts are so intense and prolonged that they actually succeed in converting ecosystems. This is what agriculture has done to forest ecosystems all over the world for centuries. Nature reserves that are not impacted by systematic human efforts to convert them could become the vehicle to preserve the evolution of biodiversity. The problem with such reserves

---

140 John Eberlee, "Assessing the Benefits of Bioprospecting in Latin America," Jan. 21, 2000 (International Development Research Center, 2001), available online at *http://www.idrc.ca/reports/read_article_english.cfm?art_num=609.*

is that they are often established under gross violations of human rights and without tolerance for any use, even traditional use, that actually benefits the reserve.

*Landscapes:* Landscapes that are tolerant of human habitation/use are an alternative way to protect biodiversity without alienating the people who make a living out of it. While landscape management is not free of conflicts, it starts from the premise that humans and nature can coexist, and thus it is preferable from both a biodiversity protection and a human rights viewpoint.

### *Privatization of Wildlife*

Privatization of wildlife has done wonders for the preservation of endangered species. As analyzed above, endangered species have rebounded dramatically under privatization efforts in Zimbabwe, Namibia, and South Africa.

### *Restoration and Gene Banks*

Gene banks and restoration are becoming the future means of protecting biodiversity, but they are limited in what they can do in terms of regenerating ecosystems lost, as some would desire. Regenerating ecosystems lost is not always feasible and many times not even socially desirable, and emphasis must be placed on restoring the productivity of ecosystems and on supporting ecosystems that can sustain themselves in the long-term. Supporting the development of stable and productive ecosystems is the purpose of restoration.

Gene banks can help bring back species that may have disappeared during wars or simply because the farmers have chosen to neglect them to concentrate on more productive species. Gene banks also could get more involved in the protection of wild species with known useful properties. In general, as "natural habitats" disappear, gene banks could become instrumental in the protection of a great amount of biodiversity whose properties are deemed worthy of protection.

International biodiversity management policies must take into account the shortcomings and advantages of all the biodiversity protection methods and must allow for the use of a wide range of tools to encourage restoration, prevention of conversion and gene bank development. Biodiversity protection policies must be based on the admission that "not all biodiversity can be 'saved' as is" and that conversion must be allowed in many instances to accommodate for the needs of the poor in the developing world.

In more detail, it is proposed that:

- Privatization and local management of protected landscapes based on human dignity values must be preferable over secluded nature reserves;
- Gene bank management must be supported further on an international scale;
- Restoration must be acknowledged as a legitimate method of biodiversity management.

As the human population increases, the future of biodiversity protection is not in segregating the land but in integrating it to produce the optimal amount of benefits. Such benefits have to include the satisfaction of the immediate needs of humans who live in biodiversity areas. People have managed and will continue to manage ecosystems to produce what they desire: wildlife, timber, recreation and agriculture. It is impossible to conceive of ecosystems that are not or will not be managed intensively to satisfy human needs.

# Chapter 3
# International Rules for National Conservation

## 1. INTERNATIONAL TREATIES FOR BIODIVERSITY PROTECTION: THE TRIUMPH OF NATIONALISTIC CONSERVATION

All international and regional instruments on biodiversity protection have the following characteristics:

- They contain vague clauses so as to give states wide latitude in balancing environmental and development considerations.
- They focus on *in situ* conservation as the best means of biodiversity protection.
- They do not use human dignity values to evaluate biodiversity protection policies.
- They rarely mention gene banks or restoration.
- They impose restrictions and prohibitions but leave it up to states to decide about the appropriate level of enforcement.
- They lack effective monitoring mechanisms to check the actual enforcement and implementation by the states.[1]
- Most of the pre-UNCED[2] instruments focus on specific regions, species and habitats. The Convention on Biological Diversity[3] was the first treaty to address biodiversity as a global matter. The Biodiversity Convention was adopted in 1992 during the UNCED conference.

---

1 This is why some states decide to strictly enforce the treaties while other states are less than willing to devote resources to enforcement.

2 The United Nations Conference on Environment and Development (UNCED) that took place in 1992 provided the impetus for the adoption of new instruments that renewed the focus on conservation.

3 Convention on Biological Diversity, June 5, 1992, *reprinted in* 31 *I.L.M.* 826 (1992).

*State Sovereignty*

All conventions, including the recently adopted Biodiversity Convention,[4] give states latitude on how to deal with conservation. States, which are the ultimate decisionmakers in the international sphere, are unwilling to release control over their natural resources to international institutions. It is not surprising then that most international treaties are vague and, despite the occasional use of stringent language, full of exceptions that increase the state's decisionmaking authority. For instance, the Convention on the Conservation of European Wildlife and Natural Habitats, known as the Bern Convention,[5] provides that states can make exceptions to the provisions of the treaty "in the interests of public health and safety, air safety or other overriding public interests."[6] A similar article is included in the African Convention[7] that allows for the killing or hunting of endangered species under government authorization in accordance with the national interest.[8] In certain cases, treaties on conservation become the pretext for coordinating development in a region. Such is the Treaty for Amazonian Cooperation.[9]

Nationalism was also obvious during the 1992 UNCED proceedings when a Convention on Forests was put on the negotiating table. Developing countries balked at the efforts to adopt a forest convention. Since forests reside in national territories, a forest convention was deemed too intrusive into the national affairs, especially if that convention were to focus on the deforestation in the developing world. Eventually, a set of Principles was adopted on the protection of all

---

4 *Id.*

5 Convention on the Conservation of European Wildlife and Natural Habitats, Sept. 19,1979, European Treaty Series No. 104, *reprinted in* IV *European Conventions and Agreements* 181 (Council of Europe ed., 1993).

6 Art. 9(1).

7 African Convention on the Conservation of Nature and Natural Resources, Sept. 15, 1968, 1001 U.N.T.S. 3.

8 Art. VII.

9 Treaty for Amazonian Cooperation, July 3, 1978, *reprinted in* 17 *I.L.M.* 1045 (1978).

forests.[10] The Principles affirm the sovereignty of countries over their natural resources.[11]

The only instruments that derogate from nationalistic conservation are the Leipzig Declaration and the Global Action Plan adopted by the FAO with regard to agrobiodiversity.[12] Within the international system, while diversity in general is the preoccupation of the United Nations Environment Program (UNEP) agrobiodiversity is the prerogative of the FAO.

The Global Action Plan adopted by the FAO is heavily influenced by the Biodiversity Convention, at least, in oratory. Nevertheless it often opts for international biodiversity management. For instance the Plan promotes international cooperation in disaster situations and encourages the safeguarding of biodiversity resources in international gene banks. The Plan clearly recognizes that the evaluation, regeneration and characterization of the collections located in gene banks cannot be accomplished without international cooperation and the economies of scale put together by international efforts.[13]

### *Structure*

Most conventions share the same structure. Conventions that deal with the protection of species do so by classifying the species in annexes. Annex I usually includes the species about to become extinct, Annex II the species under the threat of extinction and Annex III species under

---

10 Statement of Principles for a Global Consensus on the Management, Conservation and Sustainable Development of All Types of Forests, June 5, 1992, A/CONF.151/26 (Vol.II), *reprinted in* 31 *I.L.M.* 881 (1992).

11 Preamble (e), Art. 1(a).

12 The Leipzig Declaration and Global Action Plan for the Conservation and Utilization of Plant Genetic Resources for Food and Agriculture were adopted by the International Technical Conference on Plant Genetic Resources in Leipzig, Germany, June 17–23, 1996, available online at *http://www.fao.org/WAICENT/FAOINFO/AGRICULT/AGP/AGPS/GpaEN/Gpatoc.htm.*

13 *See also* the Interrelationship between the Convention on Biological Diversity and the Promotion of Sustainable Agriculture, *reprinted in* 31 *I.L.M.* 842 (1992).

threat in specific countries.[14] Some conventions provide that specific agreements need to be adopted later for the preservation of specific species. For example, under the umbrella of the Convention on Migratory species, six agreements have been adopted that are dedicated to the preservation of specific species.[15]

Treaties on the preservation of habitats are usually structured around the lists of the habitats to be protected. The World Heritage Convention[16] includes two lists: the "World Heritage List" where nature reserves are to be listed, and the "List of World Heritage in Danger." But state consent is required for the inclusion of a state territory in any of these lists.[17] The purpose of the convention is not to abdicate state sovereignty and property rights over Heritage Sites. It is to direct international cooperation to the conservation of natural heritage sites through the training

---

[14] This is the structure of the CITES Convention. *See* Convention on International Trade in Endangered Species of Wild Fauna and Flora (CITES), Mar. 6, 1973, *reprinted in* 12 *I.L.M.* 1085 (1973). The African Convention has a similar structure. Species belonging in Class A "shall be totally protected" throughout the territory unless the national interest is at stake. Class B species will also be "totally protected" but could also be hunted, killed, captured or collected (Art. VIII), *supra* note 7.

The Bern Convention includes three Annexes. The exploitation of Annex I species is totally prohibited. Annex II prohibits "the deliberate" destruction of the species. While under Annex III species are to be regulated to keep their populations out of danger, *supra* note 5.

[15] The Convention on the Conservation of Migratory Species of Wild Animals, June 23, 1979, *reprinted in* 19 *I.L.M.* 15 (1980), provides that migratory species that are endangered must be included in Annex I. Annex II is to include species of an unfavorable conservation status. Annex II species should be protected by specific agreements (Arts. III–IV). The convention provides guidelines on what these agreements must include such as monitoring and enforcement mechanisms and the maintenance of a network of suitable habitats and procedures to suppress illegal taking (Art. V). The agreements that have been adopted attempt to protect: seals in the Wadden Sea; bats in Europe; small cetaceans of the Baltic and the North Seas; Western and Central Asian Populations of the Siberian crane; slender-billed curlews; and African-Eurasian migratory waterbirds.

[16] UNESCO Convention for the Protection of the World Cultural and Natural Heritage, Nov. 21, 1972, *reprinted in* 11 *I.L.M.* 1358 (1972).

[17] Art. 11.

of specialists, interest-free loans and the establishment of a World Heritage Fund that provides financial assistance to countries in need.[18]

The list structure is also followed by the Ramsar Convention,[19] which provides that each state must designate suitable wetlands[20] for inclusion in the List of Wetlands of International Importance.[21] The Conference of the Parties has already designated 750 sites for conservation—more than 500,000 kilometers (the size of France or Kenya) of wetland.[22]

The 1992 European Union Directive follows the list structure.[23] The Directive establishes an ecological network of special areas of conser-

---

18 *See* arts. 6(1), 7, 22, 15. The fund established under the convention is very small and cannot meet the needs of developing countries.

19 Convention on Wetlands of International Importance (known as Ramsar Convention), Feb. 2, 1971, *reprinted in* 996 U.N.T.S. 245.

20 The definition of wetlands is quite broad. According to Article 1:

> For the purpose of this Convention wetlands are areas of marsh, fend, peatland or water, whether natural or artificial, permanent or temporary, with water that is static or flowing, fresh, blackish or salt, including areas of marine water the depth of which at low tide does not exceed six meters.

21 Art. 2(5).

22 Conference of the Parties to the Convention on Biological Diversity, Cooperation Between the Convention on Wetlands of International Importance, Especially as Waterfowl Habitat (Ramsar Convention) and the Convention on Biological Diversity, Sept. 23, 1996, UNEP/CBD/COP/3/30, at 3.

23 Council Directive 92/43 EEC of 21 May 1992 on the conservation of natural habitats and of wild flora and fauna, July 22, 1992, OJ L 296. Other directives that have been adopted within the context of the European Union are: the 78/409/EEC Council Directive of 2 April 1979 on the conservation of wild birds, April 2, 1979, OJ L 103. This directive was amended by Council Directive 94/24/EC of 8 June 1994 amending Annex II to the Directive 79/409/EEC on the conservation of wild birds, June 8, 1994, OJ L 164. *See also* Council Regulation (EEC) No. 3626/82 of 3 December 1982 on the implementation in the Community of the Convention on International Trade in Endangered Species of Wild Flora and Fauna, Dec. 3, 1982, OJ L 384.

Other instruments include a Regulation that deals with conservation, characterization, collection and utilization of genetic resources in agriculture. According to the Regulation, the term "agriculture" must be read broadly to include genetic resources

vation in the European Union.[24] It provides criteria (Annex III) according to which countries are to judge which of their habitats (Annex I) and which of their species (Annex II) need protection. Furthermore, the Commission in agreement with member states is to establish areas of Community importance that member states must designate as "special conservation areas."[25] Projects with negative environmental implications will be allowed in these areas only "for imperative reasons of overriding public interest, including those of a social or economic nature."[26]

### *The Human Dignity Standard/Other Standards*

Most pre-UNCED treaties do not even mention indigenous peoples' rights and make no efforts to reconcile biodiversity protection and human needs except for the African Convention that, in a limited fashion, recognizes the need to respect the customary rights of people. The African Convention provides that conservation measures should be taken with due regard to the best interests of people[27] and that states must take measures to reconcile customary rights with the goals of the convention.[28] But the convention exhibits paternalistic overtones when it mentions that states must ensure that their people understand the need and rules for the rational utilization of resources.

After the 1992 United Nations Conference on Environment and Development, international instruments seem to be more cognizant of

---

in forestry. According to Article 1(b), plant genetic resources can include, *inter alia*, "ornamental crops, medicinal plants and aromatics, fruit crops, forest trees, fungi, micro-organisms and wild flora which are or could be of use in the field of agriculture." *See* Council Regulation (EC) No 1467/94 of 20 June 1994 on the conservation, characterization, collection, and utilization of genetic resources in agriculture, June 28, 1994, OJ L 159.

24 Directive 92/43, Art. 3, *supra* note 23.

25 *Id.*, Arts. 4, 6.

26 Art. 6(4), *id.*

27 African Convention, *supra* note 7, Art. II.

28 *Id.*, Art IX.

the need to incorporate some sort of recognition of the indigenous peoples' contributions to biodiversity protection. For instance, the Forest Principles recognize that it is important for indigenous peoples to maintain their cultural identity and social organization.[29] And the Biodiversity Convention recognizes the rights of indigenous peoples in their knowledge.[30] But none of the treaties, pre- or post-UNCED, endorse human rights standards as the benchmark standards of biodiversity protection efforts.

In addition to the lack of human rights standards, most treaties lack specific standards for biodiversity protection. The lack of such standards is justified by the fact that standard making in biodiversity management is by nature more of a national/local activity than an international activity. The lack of standards, though, makes the monitoring and enforcement of the conventions quite difficult.

### *Monitoring/Implementation*

The monitoring of international treaties is often left to a Conference of Parties and a Secretariat to which states report their conservation efforts.[31] But even treaties that provide for such follow-up mechanisms are inadequately monitored. Treaties do not contain standards that will help measure the success of states in implementing them, and states are often reluctant to report information relating to biodiversity protection

---

[29] Forest Principles, *supra* note 10, Art. 5(a).

[30] Convention on Biological Diversity, *supra* note 3, Art. 8(j).

[31] The ASEAN agreement provides for a Conference of Parties and a Secretariat (Arts. 21,22, 28.) *See* Agreement on the Conservation of Nature and Natural Resources adopted by the Association of South East Asian Nations, July 9, 1985, Center for Science Information Network, *Environmental Treaties and Resource Indicators*, available online at *http//sedac.ciesin.org/entri*. The Ramsar Convention (Arts.6–8) provides also for a Conference of Parties and a Secretariat, *supra* note 19. The Convention on the Conservation of Migratory Species and Wild Animals provides for the establishment of a Conference of the Parties (Art. VII), a Secretariat (Art. IX) and a Scientific Council (Art. VII), *supra* note 15. The most comprehensive monitoring mechanism is provided under the Bern Convention, *supra* note 5. The convention establishes a Standing Committee that is charged with the monitoring of the convention (Art. 13).

either because they do not have the means to collect it or because biodiversity protection is not of a priority status in their agenda. The lack of specific standards and monitoring has made it difficult to fulfill the promises to protect biodiversity. For instance many of the sites included in the "World Heritage List" have deteriorated to such an extent that they are only by name "World Heritage Sites."[32]

The only convention that is closely monitored is the CITES Convention which deals with the trade in endangered species. According to the treaty, merchants can trade endangered species or their body parts only if they meet certain requirements and obtain permits. These requirements become the more stringent the more endangered the species are. But again the effectiveness of the treaty has been marred by too many exceptions and reservations,[33] permit falsifications, and the inexperience and lack of training of the customs personnel. Prohibitions of trade under the treaty have been defeated by a lucrative black market that has benefited from its links to organized crime. Wildlife smuggling is worth $5 billion per year.[34]

Proposals on prohibitions on timber trade are likely to generate similar outcomes. It has been proposed that developed countries must ban tropical timber imports from developing countries to save the tropical forests. It has also been proposed that if a total ban is unacceptable a partial ban on the trade of "unsustainably" collected timber could be imposed.[35] But both a total ban and a partial ban present significant problems.

Whether timber has been harvested sustainably depends on the harvesting method applied. Given the large number of timber concessions, monitoring harvesting methods will be costly domestically and almost

---

32 Jim Thorsell, "From Strength to Strength," in *World Heritage Twenty Years Later* 19, 22 (IUCN ed., 1992).

33 Reservations on provisions protecting specific species essentially legitimize trade in species otherwise protected under the convention. *See* CITES Convention, *supra* note 14, Arts. XXIII, X.

34 Renee Schaible Lewis, *Illegal Trade in Wildlife and Wildlife Products*, available online at *http://www.ecobridge.org/content/s_ill.htm*.

35 *See* Chapter 1, n.98.

impossible internationally rendering the ban ineffective. A total ban has been resisted by developing countries since timber extraction is a significant source of revenue. Considering also the current timber trade trends, a ban on timber imports into developed countries will have little effect on the overall trade. Most tropical wood in the future will be consumed in the developing world and the South-to-South trade will replace the South-to-North trade.[36] Therefore, a ban imposed by developed countries will have minimal impact on the global tropical wood consumption.

Monitoring is even more difficult under the Biodiversity Convention since many provisions of the convention are subject to different interpretations. The parties to the treaty must submit to the Conference of Parties reports on the measures taken to implement the treaty. But such reporting will be difficult, first of all, because the objectives of the treaty are not clear. Second, efforts to measure the success of biodiversity protection must be based on assessments of the existing biodiversity. Such accurate assessments do not exist.[37]

Legislation passed by the European Union, like the 1992 Directive mentioned above, is likely to be implemented more effectively than the international conventions. The member states of the European Union share a cultural cohesion and have the support of a strong institutional structure. The European Union is a *sui generis* regional organization or, for optimists, a federation. International legal instruments do not often have the level of specificity and institutional backing made possible by an entity like the European Union.

### *Biodiversity Protection Methods*

#### *Gene Banks*

Gene bank development is rarely mentioned in the pre-UNCED treaties. The instruments that focus mostly on gene bank management are those dedicated to the protection of agrobiodiversity under the auspices of the FAO. This is because a lot of agrobiodiversity is already protected in

---

36 *Id.*

37 *See infra* Section 3.

gene banks and gene banks have played a crucial role in revitalizing agricultural systems after wars and natural disasters. According to the Global Action Plan,[38] a major effort needs to be undertaken to transform the inefficient, redundant and disorganized gene bank policies into an *ex situ* conservation system. Under the Global Action Plan gene banks must not be just repositories but dynamic centers that would coordinate conservation at the national, regional and international level. The Global Action Plan calls for planned and targeted collecting efforts that will fill the gaps in existing gene banks with useful and endangered germplasm.[39]

Among the post-UNCED instruments dedicated to biodiversity protection, the Biodiversity Convention provides that gene bank development should take place preferably in the country of origin[40] reflecting nationalistic attitudes for biodiversity protection. The convention also views *ex situ* conservation as a supplemental method of *in situ* conservation rather than as a method that could take the lead role in the preservation of many species.

### *Restoration*

Similarly to gene bank management, restoration features only sporadically in pre- and post-UNCED instruments[41] more as a supplemental method of biodiversity protection rather than as an independent method that could make a difference in international efforts. For instance, in the Biodiversity Convention in the article dedicated to *in situ* conservation it is mentioned that states "shall as far as possible and as appropriate . . . [r]ehabilitate and restore degraded ecosystems and promote the recovery of threatened species, *inter alia*, through the development and implementation of plans and other management strategies."[42]

---

38 *See supra* note 12.

39 *Id.* at 27.

40 Convention on Biological Diversity, *supra* note 3, Art. 9(a).

41 *See, e.g.*, Art. 9(c), *id.*

42 Art. 8(f), *id.*

*Nature Reserves and Landscapes*

Provisions on nature reserve management are, on the contrary, prominent in most treaties. For instance, the Western Hemisphere Treaty is replete with references to "strict wilderness reserves" and obligations of state parties to "maintain the strict wilderness areas inviolate."[43] According to the ASEAN agreement,[44] nature reserves are defined as areas that "have not been substantially altered by human occupation and exploitation."[45] And the Biodiversity Convention provides that each state "shall establish a system of protected areas or areas where special measures need to be taken to protect biodiversity."[46]

The World Heritage Convention is the only convention that refers to the possibility of reconciling human use and conservation but by separating cultural sites from natural sites, it perpetuates misconceptions that nature and culture exist independently of each other. "Mixed sites" and "cultural landscapes" are today included under the scope of the convention;[47] but the proposal to include landscapes within the convention framework was met with resistance. Since landscapes exist predominantly in Europe it was believed that their inclusion in the convention would outnumber any other sites.[48]

*The Transnational Management of Transboundary Resources*

The need to manage resources transnationally is prominent in most conventions. Many treaties require state parties to consult each other if they

---

43 Art. II(1), Art. IV, Convention on Nature Protection and Wildlife Preservation in the Western Hemisphere, Oct. 12, 1940, 161 U.N.T.S. 193.

44 *See supra* note 31.

45 *Id.*, Art. 13(3)(a)(i).

46 Convention on Biological Diversity, *supra* note 3, Art. 8.

47 The World Heritage Committee, at its 10th session in December 1995 adopted 23 new cultural sites and 6 new natural sites for the World Heritage List. There are now 469 sites—350 cultural sites, 102 natural sites, and 17 mixed sites, *World Heritage Newsletter*, No. 10, Mar. 1996, available online at *http://www.unesco.org/whc/news/10newsen.htm#story4*.

48 Thorsell, *supra* note 32, at 24.

plan to create a protected area close to a common frontier.[49] Some conventions go even further and ask the parties to co-manage resources that transcend national frontiers. The Ramsar Strategic Plan of 1997–2000, for instance, advocates the development of transfrontier wetlands in accordance with Article 5 of the Ramsar Treaty.[50]

Some adjacent transnational protected areas have been declared transboundary World Heritage Sites[51] and the World Heritage Convention welcomes the designation of other such areas. Transboundary biosphere reserves have been proposed also as a way to enhance the management of national reserves.

This study supports efforts to manage resources transnationally if such efforts incorporate human dignity values. Such efforts can be private or public depending on where wildlife resides—public or private lands. The public or private transnational management of wildlife should not become the excuse, though, to suppress communities and violate human rights. A change in rhetoric—replacing the term "transboundary protected areas" with the term "transboundary landscapes"—may help reinforce perceptions that transnational management is inclusive of human habitation and manipulation.

---

49 *See, e.g.*, Art. 13(6) of the 1985 ASEAN Agreement on the Conservation of Nature and Natural Resources, *supra* note 31:

> Contracting Parties shall co-operate in the development of principles, objectives, criteria and guidelines for the selection, establishment and management of protected areas in the Region with a view to establishing a co-ordinated network of protected areas throughout the Region, giving particular attention to those of regional importance.

50 *See supra* note 19.

51 Clare Shine, "Legal Mechanisms to Strengthen and Safeguard Transboundary Protected Areas," in *Parks for Peace* 37 (International Conference on Transboundary Protected Areas as a Vehicle for International Co-operation, September 1997, Conference Proceedings, Draft of Jan. 30, 1998).

## 2. THE CITES CONVENTION AND THE BIODIVERSITY CONVENTION

The CITES Convention[52] and the Biodiversity Convention[53] constitute the cornerstones of the current international system for conservation. This system is based on prohibitions/restrictions on the trade in wildlife species and products and on the will of states to control the transfer and use of germplasm resources and technologies.

### 2.1. The CITES Convention

The CITES convention was drafted in 1963 by the International Union for the Conservation of Nature as a result of concerns that trade in wildlife was engendering huge species losses. The Convention was eventually adopted in 1973 and entered into force in 1975.

*Structure*

The structure of the CITES Convention is the same as the structure of the other conventions that deal with the threat of species loss.[54] The convention lists species in three Annexes. Annex I includes the most endangered species. Annex II includes the species threatened to become endangered. And Annex III includes endangered species in the territory of the parties to the convention. The convention prohibits the trade in species included in Annex I, regulates the trade in species included in Annex II and allows states to bring endangered species in their territory under Annex III of the convention.

According to the convention, species are traded based on import and export permit requirements that become less demanding the less strict the classification of species is. For instance, species classified in Appendix I are subject to both an import and an export permit while species classified in Appendix II are subject only to an export permit.[55]

---

[52] *See supra* note 14.

[53] *See supra* note 3.

[54] *See supra* note 14.

[55] Arts. III and IV.

*Monitoring/Enforcement*

The enforcement of the convention is left to member states. States are required to take measures to punish those who violate the convention and to confiscate items that are illegally traded or possessed.[56] States must maintain detailed records of the trade in species and share them with the Secretariat of the convention through annual reports that summarize the trade.[57] States meet also every two to three years as Conference of Parties to review the implementation of the convention and examine proposals to amend the lists of species in Appendix I and Appendix II.

The work of the Conference of Parties is facilitated by the work of four permanent committees: the Standing Committee, the Animals Committee, the Plants Committee[58] and the Nomenclature Committee.[59] The purpose of the Standing Committee is to provide assistance in implementing the convention and in overseeing the Secretariat's budget. One of the major issues that the Standing Committee has dealt with recently was whether to re-open the trade in elephant products.

Despite the mechanisms in place, the enforcement of the CITES Convention has encountered many problems. Many of the exceptions[60] to the convention, for instance, the tourist-souvenir exception[61] and the trans-shipment[62] exception and state reserva-

---

56 Art. VIII(1)(a), (b).

57 Art. VIII(7)(a).

58 The Animals Committee and Plants Committee provide specialized expertise regarding the species that are under CITES control.

59 The Nomenclature Committee was established in recognition of the need to standardize names used for animal and plant species.

60 For the exceptions to the convention and how they have been used to breach the convention, *see* Simon Lyster, *International Wildlife Law* 256–262 (1985).

61 Art. VII(3) of the Convention provides that the regulations of the convention do not apply to specimens that have personal or household effects. Some state parties apply this exception liberally—the United States for instance considers any items of personal baggage to be personal or household effects. *Id.* at 258.

62 Art. VII(1) provides that the regulations of the convention do not apply "to the transit or trans-shipment of specimens through or in the territory of a Party

tions[63] have hampered monitoring and enforcement. Exceptions have been used to smuggle species under the pretense that the exceptions apply. Reservations[64] have allowed states to opt out of the provisions of the convention and have legitimized trade otherwise considered illegal under the convention.

These loopholes, cultural beliefs that have kept up demand and a fearless network of poachers, supported by the poor of the developing world, have undermined the effectiveness of the convention. Some of the provisions of the convention, especially those regarding the bans on the trade of species and their products have hampered the people of the developing world by sabotaging local management systems. The convention has provided also the excuse to persecute those called "poachers"—in reality poor people seeking to participate in the wealth effect generated by the black markets propagated by the convention.

## 2.2. The Biodiversity Convention

The Biodiversity Convention[65] is the first attempt to deal globally with biodiversity protection. The convention is a framework convention. It does not establish biodiversity protection standards but attempts to create the outline of a regime for biodiversity protection by focusing on *in situ* conservation and marginally on restoration and gene bank management. Declaration of national sovereignty over natural resources, intellectual property rights and technology transfers become the vehicles for the establishment of such a regime. This section deals

---

while the specimens remain in Customs control." This provision has been abused since middle-men can import species from non-parties, hold them "in transit" in a state party (without, thus, having to obtain a permit) and then export them to a non-party. *Id.* at 257.

63 According to Art. XXIII(3), states that have taken reservations on certain items are considered non-parties with regard to those items. Reservations can be damaging since reserving parties often trade legally with non-parties and illegally with parties violating the letter and the spirit of the convention. *Id.* at 263.

64 Arts. XXIII, X.

65 *See supra* note 3.

extensively with the conservation aspects of the Biodiversity Convention. Chapter 4 focuses on the issues of access to biodiversity resources, transfers of technology and intellectual property rights.

Like most framework conventions, the convention reflects the concerns of its framers rather than resolves them. The convention emphasizes that states must preserve biodiversity "as far as possible and as appropriate"[66] by undertaking measures that would protect biodiversity in nature or in gene banks. But the convention never enters into the details on what states must specifically do to protect biodiversity.

### *Nationalism*

The convention places emphasis on national[67] and bilateral action based on the presumption that biodiversity can be protected more effectively at the national/bilateral level.[68] The convention clearly places biodiversity resources under national sovereignty[69] and most of its articles are

---

66 This terminology is repeated in many of the articles of the convention: Arts. 5, 6, 7, 8, 9, 10, 11, 14.

67 *See, e.g.*, Art. 6(a):

> Each Contracting Party shall, in accordance with its particular conditions and capabilities: Develop national strategies, plans or programmes for the conservation and sustainable use of biological diversity. . . .

The Second Meeting of the Conference of the Parties adopted a number of decisions that shifted the focus of the operations of the Secretariat towards the national implementation of the Convention. The Second Meeting of the Conference of the Parties voted for the creation of a clearing-house mechanism, the preparation of national reports and additional financial assistance so that countries could fulfill their obligations under the convention. *See* Conference of the Parties to the Convention on Biological Diversity, Proposed Budget of the Trust Fund for the Convention on Biological Diversity, Sept. 14, 1996, UNEP/CBD/COP/3/33.

68 Lyle Glowka et al., "A Guide to the Convention on Biological Diversity," *Environmental Policy and Law Paper No. 30* (IUCN ed., 1994).

69 Art. 15(1):

> Recognizing the sovereign rights of States over their natural resources, the authority to determine access to genetic resources rests with the national governments and is subject to national legislation.

replete with soft state obligations. Even in articles where the emphasis shifts to international cooperation, there are more allusions to national policies rather than international measures.[70] As analyzed in Chapter 4, the provisions on access to biodiversity and transfers of technology are the triumph of bilateralism.

*The International Management of Biodiversity and Human Rights*

The framers of the convention missed the opportunity to create legislation that would define the parameters of an international biodiversity management regime. Such a regime would emphasize the transnational aspects of the management of transboundary resources and international gene bank development. An international policy on biodiversity management would also make the necessary link between biodiversity protection and human rights. The convention takes into account that "the eradication of poverty is the first and overriding priority of developing countries,"[71] and recognizes the rights of indigenous peoples to their knowledge and innovations.[72] But the convention still fails to effectively link biodiversity protection with the protection of human dignity and human rights, and to present human dignity standards as the threshold standards of biodiversity protection. As mentioned before, developing

---

70 Article 5 provides that state parties must cooperate for the preservation of diversity in areas outside the national jurisdiction (for example, the high seas) or on "other matters of mutual interest" (for example, transfrontier pollution, or the regulation of migratory species). *See also* Art. 18 on Technical and Scientific cooperation. While paragraph 1 of Article 18 emphasizes the need to promote technical and scientific cooperation through the appropriate national and international institutions, paragraph 2 of the same article emphasizes:

> Each Contracting Party shall promote technical and scientific cooperation with other Contracting Parties, in particular developing countries, in implementing this Convention, *inter alia*, through the development and implementation of national policies. In promoting such cooperation, special attention should be given to the development and strengthening of national capabilities, by means of human resources development and institution building.

71 Art. 20(4).

72 Art. 8(j).

countries have defended in oratory social measures for the eradication of poverty. In practice, though, they have endorsed conservation/eco-development when it is in their interests even if that means the systematic erosion of the standard of living of the unfortunate poor within their population.

### *Gene Bank Development*

Since the convention reflects rather than attempts to alter prevalent perceptions, gene bank development plays a marginal role in biodiversity protection.[73] The convention explicitly provides that states must adopt measures of gene bank development "for the purpose of complementing *in situ* measures."[74] Gene bank development and other means of *ex situ* biodiversity protection become, therefore, a supplement to *in situ* management. It is true that gene bank development has not been used extensively for the protection of wild species. However, gene bank development certainly presents multiple possibilities for the protection of endangered species or useful wild species and it is worth exploring given the costs of nature reserve management in terms of human dignity and human rights.

The convention also provides that *ex situ* conservation measures should preferably take place in the country of origin[75] reflecting again the current nationalistic attitude toward germplasm conservation. Since most genetic resources are located in developing countries and gene banks are located in developed countries, the convention calls for an increase in the number of gene banks in the developing world. The convention also proposes that it is best for each country to have its own gene banks,[76] a too limited and not very practicable approach to germplasm preservation. Given the possibilities presented by developing regional and even international gene banks, it is not cost-efficient for many developing countries to keep their own gene banks. A

---

73 Art. 9.

74 *Id.*

75 Art. 9(a).

76 Art. 9(b).

successful example of a regional gene bank is the Nordic gene bank. While countries in other regions may not be on the friendly terms that would allow for regional gene bank development,[77] overall, regional and international cooperation is still more cost-efficient and, thus, worth pursuing. In the area of gene bank development, self-sufficiency is costly, and collaboration is certainly a more cost-effective means to conserve germplasm.[78]

### *Restoration*

The convention refers explicitly to restoration but it does so sporadically within the provisions of *in situ* and *ex situ* conservation. Clearly, according to the framers of the convention, restoration does not qualify as an independent conservation method that could make a drastic difference in international conservation efforts.[79] This short-sighted view of restoration is unfortunate since restoration could revitalize many degraded areas and thus reduce the pressure on biodiversity-rich areas. The framers of the convention could have dedicated, at least, an article of the convention solely to restoration and could have underlined that restoration is an equivalent partner of *in situ* conservation.

### *Protecting Nature Inside Nature: In Situ Conservation*

The article on *in situ* conservation presents this type of conservation as the most fundamental method of protecting biodiversity. States must "as

---

77 Donald L. Plucknett et al., *Gene Banks and the World's Food* (1987).

78 *Id.* at 191.

79 Art. 8(f):

> Each Contracting Party shall, as far as possible and as appropriate: . . . Rehabilitate and restore degraded ecosystems and promote the recovery of threatened species, *inter alia*, through the development and implementation of plans or other management strategies.

Art. 9(c):

> Each Contracting Party shall, as far as possible and as appropriate, and predominantly for the purpose of complementing *in situ* measures: . . . Adopt measures for the recovery and rehabilitation of threatened species and for their reintroduction into their natural habitats under appropriate conditions.

far as possible and as appropriate" establish a system of protected areas;[80] develop guidelines for the selection and management of protected areas;[81] regulate and manage biological resources both within and outside protected areas;[82] promote "environmentally sound and sustainable development" in areas adjacent to protected areas;[83] and adopt the necessary regulatory measures for the protection of endangered species.[84] States must also manage and control the risks associated with the release of bio-engineered organisms[85] and prevent the introduction of exotic species that may have adverse impacts on endemic species and habitats.[86]

Overall, the article on *in situ* conservation seems intentionally vague so as to give states some latitude in designing their conservation programs. Since, in practice, *in situ* conservation has meant often total preservation of protected areas based on violent evictions of the people that inhabit those areas, it would have been desirable if the provisions on *in situ* conservation included a clause that ensured that *in situ* conservation will not be pursued by violating human dignity and human rights.

It must be acknowledged, however, that the Biodiversity Convention is one of the first international treaties[87] to recognize the rights of indigenous peoples and local communities to their "knowledge," "innovations"

---

80 Art. 8(a).

81 Art. 8(b).

82 Art. 8(c).

83 Art. 8(e).

84 Art. 8(k).

85 Art. 8(g).

86 Art. 8(h).

87 Other post-UNCED agreements contain references to indigenous peoples. These references, however, sound still paternalistic. According to the Rio Declaration, indigenous peoples have a role to play in environmental conservation because "of their knowledge and traditional practices." But it is not the peoples themselves—it is the state that must support the "identity, culture and interests" of indigenous peoples. *See* Principle 22, Rio Declaration on Environment and Development, June 5, 1992, *reprinted in* 31 *I.L.M.* 874 (1992).

and "practices."[88] The Biodiversity Convention provides that the consent of indigenous peoples is needed to utilize their knowledge and that there should be equitable sharing of the benefits derived from such knowledge. The specifics of equitable sharing, though, still resist practical application.[89]

### *Implementation*

The parties must submit to the Conference of Parties the measures taken to implement the convention and an evaluation of the effectiveness of such measures in accomplishing the objectives of the convention.[90] However, such reporting is bound to be difficult not only because the objectives of the convention are far from clear but also because reporting on the effectiveness of measures to preserve biodiversity must be based on an accurate assessment of the existing biodiversity. Assessments of the current state of biodiversity—let alone "accurate assessments" —do not exist. Moreover, methodologies for measuring biodiversity are yet to be perfected. Current methods can provide an idea about the state of biodiversity resources but could not be relied upon for a comprehensive assessment. Because of the lack of an accurate methodology, most of the financial assistance to developing countries will support projects called "enabling activities"—that is the preparation of the first national biodiversity strategies and action plans that aim to assess the current status of biological diversity. The Subsidiary Body on Scientific, Technical and Technological Advice (SBSTTA)[91] has already re-emphasized that the primary focus of the assessment of biological diversity must be at the country level. However, since biodiversity does not recognize national borders and marine biodiversity is situated outside national jurisdictions some regional and international assessment will certainly become indispensable in the future.[92]

---

88 Art. 8(j).

89 *See* Chapter 4, Section 1.4.

90 *See* Arts. 26, 23(4)(a).

91 The SBSTTA was established under Article 25 of the Convention on Biological Diversity, *supra* note 3.

92 Conference of the Parties to the Convention on Biological Diversity, Third

Most current methodologies for the assessment of biodiversity are based on the measurement of species. Species, though, are often an inadequate unit for the measurement of biodiversity. In some instances the assessment of biodiversity may be more accurate in terms of phyla and families. The identification of ecosystems and habitats where biodiversity resides is even more problematic than determining the appropriate unit for measuring biodiversity. There is no universal definition of what a habitat or an ecosystem is. Attempts to classify ecosystems are based on the species that occur in them or on the physical characteristics (wetlands, forests) of the area or a combination of both. However, such classifications are in most cases incomplete descriptions of the specifics of diverse ecosystems.[93] Moreover, it is not sufficient to identify the species and habitats. Monitoring how the species and habitats change over time is equally important. Changes may involve either complete conversion or modification of habitats. Environmental modification is much more difficult to identify than conversion. For example, in the case of forests, a complete conversion of forested land into agricultural land will be easy to identify. However, partial logging may induce the multiplication of some species, the reduction of other species, or may leave the forest unaffected. The apprehension of such changes will necessitate an extensive monitoring infrastructure with a complete inventory of the species that inhabited the forest before logging. The development of such an infrastructure is labor-intensive and costly. And such an infrastructure can realistically be developed only for a small number of species.[94]

Genetic diversity, which is the focus of the Biodiversity Convention, is even more difficult to identify. Methods to measure genetic diversity require many samples and analyses by trained personnel capable of using sophisticated laboratory techniques. Because the techniques are expensive and the results produced difficult to interpret, genetic diversity is rarely used as a measure of biodiversity. The UNEP has recom-

---

Meeting, Appraisal of the SBSTTA Review of Assessments of Biological Diversity and Advice on Methodologies for Future Assessments, Sept. 13, 1996, UNEP/CBD/COP/3/13, at 4.

93 *Id.* at 6–8.

94 *Id.* at 8–9.

mended that data on biodiversity must first be collected at the species, subspecies or population level. Only biodiversity resources of economic value must be examined at the genetic level.[95]

One of the most widespread and cheapest methods to estimate biodiversity at the species level is the use of indicators. As mentioned before, the number of species even in a small area may be so great that identifying and inventorying such species will be impracticable. Certain species, therefore, can be used as indicators for the biodiversity in the whole area.[96] Actually the development of a common set of indicators could be instrumental in ensuring uniform and comparable reporting from state parties and could facilitate the administration of data under the convention.[97] The SBSTTA[98] has recommended that indicators are a feasible method for the assessment of biological diversity.

Article 7 of the Biodiversity Convention deals with the identification and monitoring of biodiversity at the national level according to a list of categories included in Annex I of the convention.[99] Some of these cat-

---

95 *Id.* at 9.

96 *Id.* at 10.

97 *Id.* at 11.

98 Art. 25.

99 According to Article 7:

> Each Contracting Party shall, as far as possible and as appropriate . . .
>
> (a) identify components of biological diversity important for its conservation and sustainable use having regard to the indicative list of categories set down in Annex 1. The categories included in Annex I are:
>
> 1. Ecosystems and habitats: containing high diversity, large numbers of endemic or threatened species, or wilderness; required by migratory species; of social, economic, cultural or scientific importance; or, which are representative, unique or associated with key evolutionary or other biological processes;
>
> 2. Species and communities which are: threatened; wild relatives of domesticated or cultivated species; of medicinal, agricultural or other economic value; or social, scientific or cultural importance; or importance for research into conservation and sustainable use of biological diversity, such as indicator species; and
>
> 3. Described genomes and genes of social, scientific or economic importance.

egories are quite vague and states will not be able to engage in identification unless some guidance is provided at the international level. For example, states will need further clarification on defining the habitats that contain "large number of species." Since the term "large number" is not further explained, and different definitions could be attached to it, states must request more detailed information about the possible interpretations of this provision.[100] Also the definition of "wilderness" will remain elusive since there are no areas on earth not impacted severely by humans.[101] It will be difficult also to identify ecosystems representative of "key evolutionary and biological processes" and ecosystems and habitats that are unique.[102] Very little is known about evolution to enable us to identify with confidence ecosystems of importance or unique ecosystems. Also no persuasive models have been developed for appraising the social, scientific and economic importance of genes and genomes.[103] However, the identification and monitoring of economically useful species must be easier and the Conference of Parties could establish priorities for the monitoring of such species.[104] It will be easier also to identify species of social, scientific or cultural importance or indicator species.[105]

Parties have to identify and monitor the activities that may have adverse impacts on biodiversity resources.[106] Identifying such activities is not easy. A change in the natural environment may be the result of many causes. It is difficult to disentangle the effects produced by natural causes from those provoked by human impacts. Moreover, the same human impacts may be appraised as both beneficial and detrimental depending on the standpoint of the observer. A human impact may

100 Conference of the Parties to the Convention on Biological Diversity, Third Meeting, Options for Implementing Article 7 of the Convention, Sept. 15, 1996, UNEP/CBD/COP/3/12, at 4 [hereinafter Assessment of 7].

101 *Id.*

102 *Id.* at 6.

103 *Id.* at 8.

104 *Id.* at 7.

105 *Id.* at 8.

106 Art. 7(c).

adversely affect certain species. On the other hand, it may contribute to the overall resilience of the ecosystem.[107]

The identification of human impacts on the environment should preferably take place before a project is undertaken. The purpose of the Environmental Impact Assessment (EIA) is exactly that: to identify the effects of human activities on nature. The convention explicitly provides that state parties must introduce "as far as possible and as appropriate" environmental impact assessments for state projects that are likely to have significant adverse impacts on biological diversity.[108] Initially EIAs were viewed as potentially useful instruments of conservation. The implementation of EIAs, however, by the World Bank, the Organization for Economic Co-operation and Development (OECD) and the European Union has revealed that EIAs have not fulfilled their potential.[109] Some of the problems with the current execution of EIAs include lack of analysis of alternative projects, mild mitigation measures, absence of monitoring and implementation, and lack of institutional capacity for competent EIA preparation. Public participation is also marginal, especially when such participation involves affected populations and local NGOs. EIAs have been especially ineffectual with regard to biodiversity-related projects since the response of ecosystems and habitats to external impacts is difficult to predict.[110]

## 3. THE INABILITY OF THE CITES CONVENTION AND THE BIODIVERSITY CONVENTION TO STEM BIODIVERSITY LOSS

To the uninitiated into international environmental law, the current international system for the protection of biodiversity seems at best contradictory: vague provisions hard to implement and difficult to enforce, selective prohibitions and restrictions not supported by consistent

---

107 Assessment of 7, *supra* note 100, at 9.

108 Art. 14(a).

109 Conference of the Parties to the Convention on Biological Diversity, Third Meeting, Note by the Executive Secretary, The Availability of Additional Financial Resources, Oct. 6, 1996, UNEP/CBD/COP/3/37, at 13.

110 *Id.*

monitoring and enforcement generating black markets all over the world. What is the point?

The point is that vague provisions, such as those included in the Biodiversity Convention, are the start-up mechanisms of international lawmaking. While they seem pointless and often conflicting, they eventually help generate agreements that include readily enforceable standards. Many successful international regimes are the product of a "framework convention" followed up by much more concrete agreements that set up clear and specific standards.[111]

It is more difficult to explain the prohibitions and restrictions with which some international instruments, such as the CITES Convention, are infused. Prohibitions and restrictions are often generated when outraged states find a certain behavior particularly despicable. It is believed that banning the behavior is the ultimate means to eradicating it. While the ban is initially vigorously monitored and enforced, even at the expense of the international human rights, it is eventually forgotten. Many new issues come up everyday in the international arena shifting the focus of states. Such issues may involve terrorism, wars, poverty and disease. It is not paradoxical, therefore, that many environmental issues, unless perceived of urgent importance, fall on the sidelines.

### *The Failure of the CITES Convention*

The CITES Convention has been unable to stem the loss of species. On the contrary it has perpetuated a lucrative black market in which many of the species are now traded. There are two basic reasons why the CITES convention has failed.

- *States are reluctant to commit the resources to back up the enforcement and monitoring of the convention*. Given the number of

---

[111] An example of such a successful regime is the regime on the Ozone Protection. *See* Vienna Convention for the Protection of the Ozone Layer, Mar. 22, 1985, *reprinted in* 26 *I.L.M.* 1529 (1987). The convention was a framework convention and was followed by a series of protocols that set explicit standards, *see, e.g.*, Adjustments and Amendments to the Montreal Protocol on Substances that Deplete the Ozone Layer, June 29, 1990, *reprinted in* 30 *I.L.M.* 537 (1991).

species protected and the methods that have been invented to smuggle such species monitoring and enforcement resources have to be substantial to support any meaningful implementation of the convention. Such resources have not been available on a consistent basis. When they have been available they have been used to apprehend and punish the poor poachers who operate on the ground rather than to dismantle the international organized crime networks.

- *The framers of the convention failed to take into account the persistent demand for certain species and their products*. This persistent demand is due to cultural attitudes that are resistant to change. Many East-Asian countries, for instance, are avid importers of body parts of endangered species, such as tigers and rhinoceros, because of their importance in traditional medicine. Some NGOs still believe that the optimal way to protect endangered species is to change the cultural attitudes of the South and view the South-East Asian dependence on traditional drugs[112] derived from endangered species as a peculiar backwardness.[113] But labeling cultural attitudes as backward has not been productive in producing compliance and has multiplied the complaints of the South against the cultural imperialism of the North.

*Interpreting the Framework of the Biodiversity Convention*

The Biodiversity Convention has not been able to stem biodiversity loss to the extent initially expected. But such expectations were doomed to

---

112 The depletion of bears is blamed on the trade in bear gallbladders used in the East for medicinal purposes. The use of the gallbladders, though, is not frivolous since it has been proved that gallbladders have medicinal value. Gallbladders produce ursodeoxycholic acid that is used in traditional Chinese medicine to cure intestinal, liver and cardiac diseases. *See* Peter Gorner, "Bears Vanishing to Feed Ethnic Medicine Market," *Chicago Tribune*, Feb. 4, 1994, at C4.

113 Shennie Patel, "The Convention on International Trade in Endangered Species,"18 *Houston Journal of International Law* 157, 208–09 (1995) (for the perspective that South-East Asians need to be educated to use alternative modern western medicines).

disappointment from the day of the adoption of the convention. This is because the convention is a framework convention that reflects states concerns about biodiversity and its exploitation for profits. It does not contain an arsenal of standards, enforcement and monitoring mechanisms to establish biodiversity protection as a priority goal. Many of the provisions of the convention concentrate on state control over natural resources and nature reserves rather than gene banks and restoration and do not propose human dignity as the standard for biodiversity protection. The convention has not been supported also with sufficient funding. But even with the adequate number of sticks and carrots, it would still be difficult for an international instrument to change the course of biodiversity conversion. As mentioned before, the deep causes of biodiversity conversion have to do with the economic conditions of the developing world and certain behavioral attitudes and beliefs that are resistant to change. Under such circumstances, the convention remains a dull affirmation of states half-hearted attempts to protect biodiversity.

The lack of current results, though, should not blind us about the future possibilities of using the convention as an instrument that could transform the face of national conservation to support the goals of international biodiversity management. The convention is flexible enough and contains elements that, with the right interpretation, could cultivate the first seeds of international biodiversity management.

Many of the provisions of the convention are flexible and because of the language used they could be interpreted to somewhat support international biodiversity management. After all the convention refers to restoration and gene bank development and recognizes the knowledge and interests of indigenous and local populations. This is far more than any other similar convention has until now recognized. Therefore, it is possible to eventually interpret the Biodiversity Convention in ways that would provide some sort of basis for international biodiversity management. A protocol to the Biodiversity Convention that would establish the link between biodiversity protection and human rights could be the first step in asserting the basic premise of international biodiversity management.

## 4. FUNDING FOR THE PROTECTION OF BIODIVERSITY

Because biodiversity has not been at the top of states' agenda for many years, it was hoped that the Biodiversity Convention would launch a new era of increased funding for the preservation of global diversity. The convention explicitly provides that "the developed country Parties shall provide new and additional financial resources to enable developing country Parties to meet the agreed full incremental costs" that they will occur in implementing the convention. This incremental assistance is to be provided in accordance with an agreement between the country and the financial mechanism—currently the GEF[114]—established under Article 21 of the Biodiversity Convention.

The hopes that the Biodiversity Convention will generate increased financial assistance for biodiversity have yet to materialize. The Organization for Economic Co-operation and Development (OECD) has revealed that funding for diversity is only a small fraction of the over-

---

114 The GEF's Operational Strategy for directing assistance for biodiversity protection has identified four operational programs:

- arid and semi-arid ecosystems;
- coastal, marine and freshwater ecosystems (including wetlands);
- forest ecosystems; and
- mountain ecosystems.

The choice of these ecosystems is in accordance with the guidance provided by the Conference of the Parties. *See* Conference of the Parties to the Convention on Biological Diversity, Third Meeting, Report of the Executive Secretary, Financial Resources and Mechanisms, Sept. 22, 1996, UNEP/CBD/COP/3/6, at 5.

The financial activities of the GEF can be classified as:

- operational programs encompassing long-term measures;
- enabling activities;
- short-term response measures.

Enabling activities are activities that constitute the foundation for the design of future effective measures. The purpose of enabling activities is to assist recipient countries to develop national strategies, plans or programs, and to identify biodiversity resources worth protecting and human activities that are likely to have adverse impacts on biodiversity. GEF projects and programs are country-driven. *See* GEF Council, Draft Report of the GEF to the Third Meeting of the Conference of the Parties to the Convention on Biological Diversity, Sept. 4, 1996, GEF/C.8/10.

all Official Development Assistance (ODA).[115] Biological diversity activities constitute only 0.75 percent of the total ODA from the period between 1987 and 1992. Only in two years, 1988 and 1992, biodiversity activities accounted for more than 1 percent of the total ODA. There was a sharp peak in biological diversity assistance in 1992. Since then, however, ODA declined to $269 million in 1993 and to $208 million in 1994.[116] The decline in assistance by bilateral and multilateral agencies and donors was only partially offset by the GEF contributions. The GEF commitment to biological diversity during the 1991–92 pilot phase was $332 million—an average of $111 million per year. However, in the year ending June 1995, the GEF assistance had fallen to $65 million, and in the year ending June 1996, it was further reduced to $23 million.[117]

These estimates, while they give a general idea about the decline in assistance for biodiversity, are not totally accurate because of the difficulties of monitoring the flows of financial assistance for biodiversity projects. No universal definition exists of what constitutes a biodiversity-related project that would facilitate the monitoring of funds channeled to biodiversity protection.[118]

Despite the propensities for miscalculation, though, it is generally agreed that the ODA for biodiversity is declining. To an extent, the

---

115 It must be noted that the OECD estimates do not include funding for the agricultural and forestry sectors and *ex situ* conservation activities. The OECD data also do not include technical cooperation and technology transfer. *See* Note by the Executive Secretary, The Availability of Additional Financial Resources, Conference of the Parties to the Convention on Biological Diversity, Third Meeting, Oct. 6, 1996, UNEP/CBD/COP/3/37, at 6.

116 *Id.* at 7.

117 *Id.* at 8.

118 Multiple methodological complexities make it difficult to estimate how much assistance has already been directed to biodiversity projects. For instance, different methods have been applied to measure "new and additional" financial assistance. Some measure additionality in terms of historical levels of ODA that existed the time the Biodiversity Convention was opened for signature. Others measure additionality in terms of the minimum targets for ODA provided by the General Assembly resolutions. Others characterize as new and additional financing, financing generated from new institutional mechanisms without reference to the overall levels of previous assistance. *Id.* at 18.

decline in assistance for biodiversity reflects the overall decline in Official Development Assistance. But, while the overall decline in ODA is only 6 percent, the decline in biological diversity-related assistance is 80 percent.[119]

The decline in funding has been attributed to the difficulties that exist in designing and implementing effective biodiversity projects. It is hard to design and implement *in situ* biodiversity projects because their success depends on the modification of human interactions with nature. This modification cannot happen instantaneously and its effects are felt only after long periods of time. But while the rate of species extinction and the overall value of biodiversity are under constant reevaluation, other conventional infrastructure projects are less complex, their costs can be easily estimated and the benefits they produce are more evident. Inevitably, therefore, they attract more funding. For instance, the benefits of a better transportation network are more readily felt than the benefits of nature preservation. It is difficult to estimate the contributions of each and every protected area to human welfare.[120]

Since Official Development Assistance is diminishing, efforts have focused on attracting foreign direct investment. Funding from non-governmental and private entities is becoming an important source for funding biodiversity-related activities.[121] Joint ventures use public funds to attract private-sector investment for projects that have a biological diversity component, for instance, ecotourism or genetic research. Several venture-capital funds for biological diversity have already been initiated.[122]

Debt-for-nature swaps, an alternative method to encourage biodiversity protection in the developing world, while promising when first ini-

---

119 *Id.* at 8.

120 *Id.* at 10–11.

121 *Id.* at 18.

122 Publicly sponsored venture-capital funds include: the Global Environment Emerging Markets Fund (US government sponsored); the Nordic Environmental Finance Corporation (sponsored by the Nordic countries) and the North American Environmental Fund (partly sponsored by the Japanese Overseas Economic Corporation Fund). *Id.* at 14.

tiated, have become less frequent. Since 1987 commercial debt has been exchanged for conservation in sixteen countries generating $129 million for biodiversity-related projects. The recipient country usually agrees to commit local funds to a biodiversity project in exchange for reducing the face value of its debt. NGOs are involved in most of the debt-for-nature transactions. NGOs usually buy the debt at a discount price in the secondary market and subsequently negotiate with the country the terms of the conversion.[123]

Debt-for-nature swaps may become easier in the future. Thirty-two developing countries have developed national environmental trust funds (NEFs). Since 1990, at least $850 million have been contributed to those funds. However, most of the resources come from bilateral and multilateral grants and only occasionally from debt-conversion plans.[124] It will be interesting to see whether in the future NEFs will be used in debt-conversion programs and whether developing countries will be willing to preserve natural resources for debt-relief purposes. Developing countries have often viewed debt-for-nature swaps as a covert method to usurp their sovereignty. A debt-for-nature conversion may mean that productive areas will have to be committed to conservation for years. Developing countries with scarce land resources keen on putting the land into productive use may eventually regret the commitment of land for debt. Environmental organizations that lack the monitoring capacity to ensure that the designated protected area is really protected may eventually become disillusioned with debt-for-nature programs.

In general, because of the difficulties in establishing the goals and baselines of biodiversity protection, and thus clearly delineate biodiversity projects, financial assistance for biodiversity is not bound to be bountiful in the future unless some kind of an emergency refocuses attention on the importance of preservation of biodiversity resources. Private assistance may increase but only for projects that are likely to produce tangible results, such as ecotourism and genetic preservation and manipulation. Such projects are a far cry from what conservationists mean when they demand increased assistance for biodiversity protection.

---

123 *Id.* at 16.

124 *Id.* at 17.

# Chapter 4
# International Rules for the Exchange of Germplasm

## 1. BILATERALISM VERSUS FREE ACCESS MULTILATERALISM

### 1.1. Background: Access to Germplasm Resources and Intellectual Property Rights

#### 1.1.1. The Seed Wars

From historical times, unimproved genetic material has been the common heritage of mankind, freely accessible to everyone.[1] Seeds have moved around the globe under the understanding that they can be freely used and exchanged. Free use, though, has not been a norm without exceptions. Colonial governments freely exchanged seeds and simultaneously prohibited the exportation of seeds lucrative for trade. The Dutch destroyed all the nutmeg and clove trees in Muluccas except for those they planted themselves so as to prevent exportation by the locals. The French made the export of indigo seeds from Antigua a capital offense.[2] Even today states often refuse to release control over the exportation of seeds that make the bulk of their export trade.

While unimproved germplasm has been generally freely available, improved germplasm produced by advanced breeding is protected under intellectual property rights and plant breeders' rights. In the 1920s and 1930s countries started to expand intellectual property protection to include plant breeders' rights.[3] The United States introduced the Plant

[1] *See* Calestous Juma, *The Gene Hunters: Biotechnology and the Scramble for Seeds* 37 (1989).

[2] Jack R. Kloppenburg Jr. & Daniel Lee Kleinman, "Plant Genetic Resources: The Common Bowl," in *Seeds and Sovereignty* 1, 5 (Jack R. Kloppenburg Jr. ed., 1988).

[3] Juma, *supra* note 1, at 154.

Patent Protection Act,[4] which permits patent rights on asexually produced plants, and the Plant Variety Protection Act, which provides protection for sexually produced plants.[5] European countries also introduced plant breeders' rights.[6] Plant breeders' rights are exclusive rights granted to breeders to prevent the unauthorized use of their varieties. Breeders' rights give breeders incentives to produce more varieties by allowing them to reap off seizable profits from their innovations. But breeders' rights also have induced tight controls on the transfers and use of improved seeds and a high concentration of the seed supplies in the hands of the powerful seed industry.

The power of the seed industry and its ability to set prices for the advanced cultivates it produces[7] set off the seed wars of the 1980s. The disputes focused on the free access policies to unmodified germplasm implemented by gene banks and the International Agricultural Research Centers. Developing countries argued that gene banks and the International Agricultural Research Centers in particular are the agents of multinational seed corporations. The International Agricultural Research Centers used to allow free access to germplasm in their collections, but the high-yielding varieties produced by seed companies by using that germplasm are quite expensive to purchase because they are protected by patents or breeders' rights. Developing countries argue that it is unfair to have to pay for these varieties that would have never been developed

---

4 35 U.S.C. § 161 (1988).

5 Plant Variety Protection Act (PVPA) of 1970, 7 U.S.C §§ 2321–2583 (1988). The protection provided by a plant patent is not as extensive as the protection granted by a utility patent. Also the standards of novelty, utility and non-obviousness are less strict for plant varieties than utility patents.

6 *See, e.g.*, Convention for the Establishment of the European and Mediterranean Plant Protection Organization, April 18, 1957, U.K.T.S. 44.

7 Out of the world's 1,500 companies 600 can be found in the United States and 400 in Europe. *See* Rabobank Nederland, "World Seed Market Faces Stagnation," Agra Europe, Aug. 26, 1994.

The development of the seed industry made possible the Green Revolution. The Green Revolution involved concentration on the production of high yielding varieties—easily reproducible plant varieties that make possible increased outputs, *see* Juma, *supra* note 1, at 79.

without the free access policies to unmodified germplasm located in international gene banks and initially discovered within their territory.

The seed wars demonstrated the unwillingness of developing countries to keep sharing their germplasm resources with multinational corporations and put in effect the adoption of a set of rules that asserted national sovereignty over germplasm resources. Seed and pharmaceutical industries, which up to the late 1980s were able to obtain germplasm from developing countries without monetary compensation, must now request permission for access and pay a fee for the use and commercialization of plant resources. Attempts by corporations to obtain seeds, isolate their properties and claim intellectual property rights over them without acknowledging and compensating the contributions of indigenous peoples have been called biopiracy.[8] Such incidents have acquired often international dimensions involving states, public and non-governmental institutions, and indigenous farmers.

In the 1950s and 1960s, the United States National Cancer Institute and Eli Lilly took an interest in folk medicines from Africa and were intrigued by the association of the rosy periwinkle of Madagascar with the treatment of diabetes. The rosy periwinkle was used originally by Malagasy healers primarily for treating diabetes. The scientists screened the plant and found two compounds that are today incorporated into powerful anti-cancer drugs. But, because of the absence of policies addressing issues of ownership and compensation none of the royalties trickled down to the Malagasy people.[9]

In 1995, more than 200 organizations from 35 countries filed a petition at the United States Patent and Trademark Office calling for the revocation of a patent given to the W.R. Grace to use a pesticide extract from the neem tree. They argued that the company has wrongfully usurped an age-old biological process used by millions of farmers in

---

[8] *See* "The Captain Hook Awards for Outstanding Achievements in Biopiracy," *News Release, Rural Advancement Foundation International* (RAFI), May 17, 2000.

[9] *Access to Genetic Resources: An Evaluation of the Development and Implementation of Recent Regulation and Access Agreements* 12 (Prepared for the Biodiversity Action Network by the Environmental Policies Study Workshop, School of International and Public Affairs, Columbia University, 1999).

India and other countries for generations. W.R. Grace was initially granted the patent because it invented a process that stabilizes the activity and increases the storage time of a compound of the neem tree called azadirachtin. The European Patent Office has recently revoked the patent.[10]

In March 1995, the Swiss Supreme Court ruled that the manzana variety of chamomile plant may not be patented. It revoked the patent that the Swiss patent office had granted in 1988 to the German pharmaceutical company Degussa/Asta Medica for its manzana variety.[11]

In February 1995, the European Patent Office withdrew key parts of a patent that was granted to a Belgian company (Plant Genetic Systems) and a United States company (Biogen Inc.) for genetically engineered herbicide resistant plants. The patent was for plant cells made resistant to glutamine synthetase inhibitors by genetic engineering. The patent originally did not cover only the gene but also all plant cells and plants containing the gene. After the challenge of the patent by Greenpeace, the Patent Office's Appeal Board ruled that the patent may only cover genetically engineered genes and plant cells but cannot extend to the whole plant, its seeds and future generations of plants grown from the cells.[12]

On December 20, 2000, the International Center for Tropical Agriculture (CIAT) filed a formal request for re-examination of a patent known as the yellow bean or "Enola bean" patent filed with the United States Patent and Trademark Office. CIAT is one of the international research centers supported by the Consultative Group on International Agriculture Research (CGIAR). A non-governmental organization, the Rural Advancement Foundation International (RAFI) had denounced the patent as "Mexican bean biopiracy" and demanded that the patent

---

10 *See* Ashok Sharma, "Tree Focuses Debate on Control of Resources," *L. A. Times*, Nov. 19, 1995, at A6; "Neem Tree Patent Revoked", *BBC News*, May 11, 2000, available online at *http://www.bbc.co.uk/hi/english/sci/tech/newsid_745000/745028.stm*.

11 Martin Khor, "A Worldwide Fight Against Biopiracy and Patents on Life," *Third World Network*, available online at *http://www.twnside.org.sg/title/pat-ch.htm*.

12 *Id.*

be legally challenged and revoked. The Enola bean patent is especially controversial because the owner and president of the seed company purchased yellow bean seeds in Mexico in 1994 and filed for an exclusive monopoly less than two years later. The company got the patent in 1999 and filed suits against two companies that were selling Mexican yellow beans in the United States. The CIAT, in its official request for re-examination of the patent, claims that the patent should not have been granted in the first placc because the requirements of novelty and non-obviousness are not met.[13]

In 2001, Greenpeace and the German Catholic Church agency filed a legal objection at the European Patent Office against a far-reaching patent obtained by DuPont.[14] The organizations accuse DuPont of biopiracy and challenge the company's claim for exclusive rights on all maize with especially high oil and oleic acid content.[15] According to the claimants, a specific method of hybridization must not grant DuPont private intellectual property rights over all varieties expressing the desired properties. Such varieties have existed naturally and have been developed by maize breeders many years ago.

Claims of biopiracy have also been made against public institutions, for instance, against the Colorado State University for patenting the Andean quinoa, against the University of California at Davis for making claims on the disease resistant rice gene of West Africa, and against the University of Wisconsin for patenting brazzein from West Africa.[16]

This climate of distrust is reflected in the international instruments that have been adopted.

---

13 "Enola Bean Patent Challenged," *RAFI News Release*, Jan. 5, 2001.

14 "Greenpeace and Misereor Challenge Dupont Biopiracy Patent," May 29, 2001, available online at *http://www.greenpeace.org/pressreleases/geneng/2001may29.html*.

15 DuPont has asked for a total control over any use of maize varieties with high oleic acid content throughout the entire production chain—from seeds to harvest and products.

16 "In Search of Higher Ground," *RAFI Occasional Paper Series*, Vol.6, No. 1, Sept. 2001.

### 1.1.2. Intellectual Property Rights Over Biodiversity Resources

Intellectual property rights are not new. They have existed since ancient times. Monopoly rights were granted to inventors as early as 200 B.C. Intellectual property rights regimes have a dual purpose: to motivate inventors by recognizing ownership over the fruits of their intellectual endeavors and to benefit the public by requiring the licensing of inventions. The rationale for the protection of intellectual property is that if inventors generate profits from their inventions, they will be more willing to engage in creative activities. The same rationale lies behind plant breeders' rights, copyrights, trademarks, patents, and other offshoots of intellectual property rights.

To receive protection under an intellectual property rights regime, the inventor has to prove novelty, an inventive step, and non-obviousness. This is the difference between a discovery and an invention. A discovery is not protected under the law because it is an abstract idea, an intangible concept, for example, the discovery of a natural force or a mathematical formula. The application of an idea to create something useful constitutes the core of an invention.[17] It is sometimes difficult to draw the line between discoveries and inventions, especially in defining what constitutes commercial application. Because of these difficulties that are even more acute in the field of biotechnology, there are so many challenges against biotechnology inventions.

#### *Plant Breeders' Rights and the UPOV Convention*

Plant breeders' rights were the first rights to be asserted over living resources. The International Union for the Protection of New Varieties of Plants, known by the French acronym as the UPOV Convention,[18] has

---

17 *See generally* Stephen A. Bent et al., *Intellectual Property Rights in Biotechnology Worldwide* 106 (1987); *See also* 35 U.S.C. § 103 (1988); Convention on European Patents, Oct. 5, 1973, *reprinted in* 13 *I.L.M.* 268 (1974).

18 The UPOV Convention was adopted in 1961 and was amended in 1978 and in 1991, *reprinted in* 815 U.N.T.S. 89. Forty countries have laws that cover plant breeders' rights. Thirty of these countries are parties to the UPOV Convention. Countries of the Andean Pact have developed their own system of plant breeders'

unequivocally established plant breeders' rights on plant varieties that are novel, uniform, distinctive and stable.[19] The 1991 amendments of the convention strengthened breeders' rights by removing the farmers' exception and leaving it up to individual countries to decide whether such an exception is appropriate for their domestic legislation. According to the prior version of the convention, farmers could save seeds protected under breeders' rights for the following year. Under the 1991 amendments, the ability of farmers to save seeds is decided by national legislation.[20] The Convention has also made it more difficult to use breeders' varieties for experimental purposes. In general the amendments try to place breeders' rights on an equal footing with patent rights. Patent rights are granted for biotechnology inventions and provide stronger protection for those inventions than the protection provided for traditional breeding. Seed industries have demanded that breeding and biotechnology be granted similar status by strengthening the legal protection provided for breeders. However, in most national laws, plant breeders' rights are still weaker than patent rights and a claim under a breeders' rights regime is subject to a less vigorous examination than a claim under a patent regime. This less vigorous examination has led sometimes to the protection of minor or cosmetic improvements giving support to complaints of biopiracy by developing countries.

---

rights. India and the Philippines are considering legislation that will provide rewards to breeders.

Member countries to the World Trade Organization will have to provide for the protection of the rights of breeders either through a patent system or a breeders' rights system. *See* Commission on Genetic Resources for Food and Agriculture, Second Extraordinary Session, Report on the State of World's Plant Genetic Resources, April 22–27, 1996, CGRFA-EX2/96/2, at 37.

19 Art. 5.

20 *See* Art. 14(1). National legislation can restrict breeders' rights and allow for the farmers' exception. *See* Art. 15(2). The United States has amended the Plant Variety Protection Act to grant an unconditional farmers' privilege to all growers of sexually propagated species. The European Union has chosen to limit the privilege to certain species and to give an unqualified privilege only to small farmers. *See* Adelaida Harris, "Why Change the UPOV Convention?" Information Meeting on the Protection of New Varieties of Plants under the UPOV Convention, UPOV/IM/96/3.

*Intellectual Property Rights over Bio-Engineered Organisms*

There is still a debate on whether intellectual property rights can be granted for the modification of living organisms and biotechnology inventions. Patent rights over biotechnology inventions are granted over innovations that involve the isolation, purification, modification or manipulation of the natural properties of a substance for future commercial application. The United States was one of the first countries to establish patent rights over biotechnology inventions.[21] In order to receive protection for biotechnology devices, the inventor has to prove novelty, an inventive step, and non-obviousness.[22]

Intellectual property rights over biotechnology inventions have now the backing of the International Trade Organization. The international Trade Related Intellectual Property Rights (TRIPs) agreement,[23] provides that countries can recognize patents on most products and processes including pharmaceuticals, modified microorganisms, and microbiological processes. Countries can protect also plant varieties under patents or other *sui generis* systems. The agreement thus gives countries some sort of discretion in deciding whether patents or other rights must be granted to "essentially biological processes for the production of plants or animals."[24] While there are exceptions to the agreement,[25] they are likely to be strictly interpreted and are unlikely to provide a subterfuge for derogating from the spirit of the agreement, which gives full protection to intellectual property rights over living organisms.

---

21 The first court decision that established intellectual property rights over biotechnology in the United States is *Diamond v. Chakrabarty*, 447 U.S. 303 (1980).

22 *See* 35 U.S.C. § 103 (1988); Convention on European Patents, Oct. 5, 1973, *reprinted in* 13 *I.L.M.* 268 (1974).

23 TRIPs Agreement, Annex IC of the Marrakesh Agreement Establishing the World Trade Organization, April 15, 1994, available online at *http://www.wto.org/english/tratop_e/trips_e/t_agmo_e.htm*.

24 Art. 27.3(b).

25 According to Art. 27.2, countries may refuse to grant patents when it is necessary to protect public order or morality, human, animal and plant life or health or to avoid adverse environmental effects. But the refusal cannot be based on the fact that the national health and safety regulations of the country have yet to approve the product or process.

The issue of intellectual property rights over biotechnology was discussed extensively during the adoption of Biodiversity Convention. Developing countries have demanded "the equitable sharing of benefits" coming from biotechnology inventions developed by using their germplasm resources. But what "equitable sharing" means is still unclear. Article 16(1) & (3) require each party to facilitate access to the technology of the other party "on mutually agreed terms." But Article 16(2) provides that technology transfers cannot violate recognized intellectual property rights.[26] Thus the convention seems to honor bilateralism based on the protection and respect for intellectual property rights.

### 1.2. The Convention on Biological Diversity: Bilateral Agreements for Access to Plant Genetic Resources

The Biodiversity Convention[27] has given states the final authority regarding the dissemination of natural germplasm located within national borders. The genetic resources covered under the convention are not inclusive of the resources acquired before the entry into force of the convention.[28] Resources preserved before the entry into force of the convention include the most profitable resources safeguarded in the International Agricultural Research Centers and other gene banks. The non-retroactive application of the Biodiversity Convention has created a two-tiered system for the transfer of resources: *de facto* free access to gene bank resources acquired before the entry into force of the Biodiversity Convention, and restricted access to all other resources. The issue of free access to pre-Convention resources is now addressed through the International Treaty on Plant Genetic Resources for Food and Agriculture.

The Biodiversity Convention provides that no access to natural resources will be allowed without some equitable sharing of the benefits

---

26 Article 16(5) also provides that intellectual property rights must be "supportive of" and must not "run counter" to the objectives of the convention. But the objectives of the convention are vague and do not resolve conclusively what "equitable sharing means."

27 Convention on Biological Diversity, June 5, 1992, *reprinted in* 31 *I.L.M.* 826 (1992).

28 Art. 15(3).

derived from the manipulation of resources. According to the convention, unrestricted access to germplasm resources cannot take place without a prior agreement on the equitable sharing of technology that manipulates the resources—that is biotechnology. This provision, which calls for bilateral agreements regarding the transfer of resources and technologies, has provoked the opposition of the biotechnology industry that is reluctant to share its applications with developing countries and has prevented the United States from ratifying the convention.[29]

The Biodiversity Convention has given the green light to countries to adopt legislation that would provide procedures for access to their resources. To honor the bilateralism supported by the convention, countries now require bioprospectors to provide a letter of intent including the number of specimens required, the manner of collecting those specimens, and their final destination. In some cases it is not only the national consent that is required, but also the local and indigenous

[29] The Biodiversity Convention specifically provides for the sharing of benefits derived from access to germplasm resources. The sharing of benefits requirement links the provisions on access to germplasm with the provisions on transfers of technology and financial assistance. These provisions are difficult to interpret because they are reflective of the disagreements that prevailed during the negotiations of the convention. According to the convention, unrestricted access to genetic resources should not be granted without a prior agreement on the equitable sharing of the technology that manipulates the resources—that is biotechnology. *See* Art. 15(3). Article 16 of the convention is centered on the proposition that developed countries can obtain access to biodiversity resources under the condition that they provide access to biotechnology. This conditional access to biodiversity resources, the United States industry claims, could lead to compulsory licensing of biotechnology inventions. Article 16 has been the primary reason why the United States has refused to ratify the Biodiversity Convention. The Clinton interpretative statement paid particular attention to intellectual property rights. The Clinton Administration stressed that the sharing of benefits must take into account "the exclusive rights to technology that a party may possess" and that transfers of technology can take place "only at the discretion of the owner of technology." The Clinton statement also declared that resources "obtained by public and private entities before the Convention enters into force or obtained outside of its scope are not governed by the Convention." *See* Statement of the President of the United States on the Convention on Biological Diversity, 103rd Congress, 1st Session, Treaty Document 103–20, US Government Printing Office (1993).

communities consent.[30] Countries adopted this type of restrictive regulations in the hope of enriching themselves by using their germplasm resources. This type of legislation, though, has not brought wealth to the South and has unnecessarily curbed the interest of the North in unexplored resources. As some commentators have put it, bioprospecting "profits have been elusive, and win-win opportunities have been few and far between."[31] According to the same commentators, technology transfers and capacity building are the most countries should expect from bioprospecting agreements. Bioprospecting agreements will bring rarely to developing countries the "green gold" they initially hoped for.

Today few countries have tried to ensure that preconditions for access to their resources do not amount to prohibitions and that access to germplasm resources remains more or less unencumbered. In order to allow for the unencumbered access to resources, some countries have opted for:

- bioprospecting agreements that include as many stakeholders as possible coupled with legal devices that reduce the complexity of dealing with many stakeholders simultaneously;[32]

---

[30] Most national laws today usually distinguish between commercial and academic research even if the borderline between these two types of research is often blurred, for instance, when a corporation is funding the research program of an academic institution. *See* Conference of the Parties to the Convention on Biological Diversity, Third Meeting, 4–15 November 1996, UNEP/CBD/COP/3/20, at 13 (Oct. 5, 1996) [hereinafter National Legislation]; Ana Sittenfeld & Rodrigo Gamez, "Biodiversity Prospecting by INBio," in *Biodiversity Prospecting: Using Genetic Resources for Sustainable Development* 69, 82 (Walter V. Reid et al. eds., 1993).

[31] *Access to Genetic Resources: An Evaluation of the Development and Implementation of Recent Regulation and Access Agreements* v (Prepared for the Biodiversity Action Network by the Environmental Policy Studies Workshop, School of International and Public Affairs, Columbia University ed., 1999).

[32] In order to reduce the parties who negotiate with a foreign organization some countries have opted for overlapping agreements: one between the state and the national organization and the other between the national organization and the foreign organization. Such overlapping agreements provided the framework for the famous Merck-INBio cooperation. *Id.* at 23.

- bioprospecting arrangements in areas where property rights are clear—namely state parks and other protected areas;[33]
- flexibility. Many agreements, for instance, distinguish between commercial and non-commercial research;
- technology transfers and capacity building rather than large inflows of cash compensation.

Despite the fact that it is flexibility and realism about the returns that bring countries and companies to the negotiating table, most countries are still looking for the "green gold." For instance, in Colombia, Bio-Andes, a biotechnology corporation, was unable to obtain access because of the insurmountable number of bureaucratic requirements imposed by the Colombian Ministry of the Environment.[34] And in the Philippines only two out of thirty-seven applications have been approved for bioprospecting since 1995.[35]

Eventually countries will have to lower barriers to bioprospecting when they realize that many of the chemicals that interest biotechnology firms do not reside in one country or in one species but are actually shared among many countries and species.[36] Because genetic diversity

---

33 Because agreements target already protected areas, they have not been instrumental in increasing the number of areas under protection, *id.* at iii.

34 Andes Pharmaceuticals is a company that was formed in 1993 as a response to the Convention on Biological Diversity to use biodiversity in developing countries and to transfer technology to those countries. The repeated applications of Andes Pharmaceuticals for access to the biodiversity resources of Colombia were rejected, though, for what seem to be arbitrary reasons. Andes Pharmaceuticals has reportedly incurred $1 million in transaction costs in its attempts to get access to Colombia's biodiversity resources. Andes Pharmaceuticals has decided not to operate anymore in the Andean Pact countries. Another two requests for access have been made in Colombia. A request was made by a Colombian researcher operating from Germany who quitted after realizing how lengthy and costly the application process is. The other request by a local researcher has yet to be resolved. *Id.* at 43.

35 *Id.* at iv.

36 Joseph Henry Vogel, *Bioprospecting* (Final Report, Commissioned by the Biodiversity Support Program on behalf of the Inter-American Commission on Biodiversity and Sustainable Development in preparation for the Summit of Americas on Sustainable Development, Santa Cruz de La Sierra Bolivia, Dec. 6–8, 1996).

is rarely unique to a country or a species, companies pay less attention to the species and focus on the compounds that make them—compounds that are usually common in many species within a region. For instance, the biological diversity in Costa Rica is not unique to Costa-Rica but is shared by the other countries in the region. So when Costa Rica gives access to its resources, it actually gives access to the resources of the whole region.

The low value attributed to the collection of species in comparison to the isolation of a profitable compound from a known useful species is reflected in the amount of royalties agreed in bioprospecting contracts. In many contracts royalties are reported to be as low as 0.2 percent of net sales. Even INBio in Costa Rica is believed to be receiving royalties as low as 2 percent of net sales.[37]

In order to ensure benefits from germplasm exploitation and to diminish the possibility of relentless competition among the countries endowed with more or less the same resources, states have enacted regional rules for access to resources.[38] It is hoped that this cartel-like behavior would bridge the disparate interests and discourage free-rider behavior.

Cartel organizations, however, are not always successful in curbing the free rider problem as the OPEC experience demonstrates. Moreover, germplasm resources are quite dissimilar from oil resources. As mentioned above, markets for germplasm of untested quality do not exist the way markets for oil exist. In addition, a too restrictive national/regional system could isolate a country/region from the networks of seed exchange and information. If a country/region restricts access to its genetic resources, it should expect a similar response from other countries. A nationalistic view of germplasm could threaten international cooperation that is vital for biodiversity protection.

Bioprospecting agreements or Material Transfer Agreements (MTAs), while not very profitable, are becoming the future means for transferring

---

37 *Id.* at 4.

38 Andean Community, Decision 391: Common Regime on Access to Genetic Resources, July 1996, available online at *http://www.sice.oas.org/trade/JUNAC/decisiones/DEC391e.asp*. The countries in the cartel include Bolivia, Colombia, Ecuador, Peru, and Venezuela.

germplasm. MTAs could allow for access while prohibiting any intellectual property rights over the germplasm, could allow for the assertion of intellectual property rights under an obligation to share the royalties, or could leave contentious matters to future negotiations.

But the minimal profits brought by the MTAs raise the question whether it is cost-effective to enter such agreements. The minimal benefits brought by MTAs could be drained by the legal and administrative costs involved in negotiating benefit-sharing.

Because of the high costs of negotiating and enforcing MTAs in comparison with the benefits, MTAs are relatively rare. To avoid the costs associated with bilateral MTAs' negotiations, it has been proposed that a multilateral system for the transfer of germplasm is needed.[39] Such a system was adopted for the food and agriculture resources in 2001 after years of negotiations under the umbrella of the Treaty on Plant Genetic Resources for Food and Agriculture. If this treaty is ratified and gradually improved to encompass all useful species and other species that may be of value, it could provide a relief for the bilateralism that plagues the international system and threatens food security.

Beyond the cost-benefit evaluation of MTAs, fundamental questions can be raised about the type of development that can be achieved through MTAs. It is arguable whether the type of development propagated by these agreements will help developing countries exit the stage of "dependent development." For instance, the INBio functions because of the infusion of money from a large company of the North—money that may dry out any moment Merck decides that the INBio does not serve its objectives. Bioprospecting, like export agriculture, depends heavily on the economic prospects of the North and cannot address the roots of the economic problems of the South.

---

[39] Access to Plant Genetic Resources and the Equitable Sharing of Benefits 33 (Issues in Genetic Resources, No. 4, a feasibility study prepared by IPGRI, June 1996) ("[t]o negotiate specific benefit-sharing arrangements with every country of origin will be daunting. To negotiate with individual farmers or communities will be virtually impossible. The enormous costs of such negotiations and the implementation of multiple benefit-sharing arrangements would almost certainly result in a drastic reduction of the use of new germpalsm.").

Developing countries must not rely on MTAs solely to take advantage of their germplasm. They need to develop their screening potential and eventually their biotechnology potential. It is easier for developing countries to enter the field of biotechnology than, for example, to master microelectronics.[40] The entry barriers into the biotechnology field are not that high especially for mastering traditional methods such as tissue culture. India is developing an expertise in biotechnology. Research institutes in the Southern Indian City of Bangalore have made impressive progress in biotechnology.[41]

## 1.3. The Treaty on Plant Genetic Resources for Food and Agriculture: Toward a Multilateral System for Access to Plant Genetic Resources

The Treaty on Plant Genetic Resources for Food and Agriculture was adopted after nine years of negotiations on November 3, 2001.[42] The treaty has its roots in the International Undertaking on Plant Genetic Resources.

The International Undertaking on Plant Genetic Resources was one of the first instruments to deal with germplasm resources for food and agriculture and it was not a legally binding instrument. In the 1983 version of the Undertaking it is mentioned that plant genetic resources are a heritage of mankind and should be available without restriction.[43] The Undertaking was modified in 1989 to clarify that "free access does not mean free of charge."[44] It was modified also in 1991 to clarify that the

---

40 *See* Juma, *supra* note 1, at 176.

41 Fred Powledge, "Who Owns Rice and Beans?" 45(7) *Bioscience* 440, July 1995. *See also* Ganapati Mudur, "New Rules Push Researchers Closer to Biotech Industry," 269 *Science* 297 (No. 5222), July 21,1995.

42 International Treaty on Plant Genetic Resources for Food and Agriculture, Nov. 3, 2001, adopted by the FAO Conference, available online at *ftp://ext-ftp.fao.org/waicent/pub/cgrfa8/iv/ITPGRe.pdf.*

43 Art. 1, Resolution 8/83, Twenty-Second Session, FAO Conference, Nov. 5–23, 1983.

44 Resolution 4/89, Twenty-Fifth Session, FAO Conference, Nov. 11–29, 1989. The amended Undertaking also recognized plant breeders' rights, first recognized internationally under the UPOV Convention, *supra* note 18.

principle that genetic resources are the heritage of mankind is subject to the "sovereignty of states over plant genetic resources."

After the adoption of the Biodiversity Convention—which subjected the transfers of germplasm to bilateral controls—the need to clarify the status of agricultural and food resources that were freely exchanged for years became obvious. At issue here were the resources kept in the International Agricultural Research Centers. These resources were collected before the Biodiversity Convention and were considered to be *de facto* free access resources. The gene banks of the International Agricultural Research Centers contain 35–40 percent of world's unduplicated collections.

A new version of the Undertaking was put forward on July 1, 2001,[45] but many important provisions were still bracketed. For instance, the list of crops that would be free access was still debated. Some developing countries wanted to keep crops off the list in the hope of making money by charging fees bilaterally for access to those seeds.[46] Also patents on derived material were allowed but that provision was still bracketed.[47] Another bracketed provision emphasized that the International Undertaking is subordinate to the World Trade Organization, meaning that the provisions regarding the protection of intellectual property adopted by the World Trade Organization would prevail if in conflict with the provisions of the International Undertaking.[48]

The negotiations on a new mandate for the International Undertaking progressed at a very slow pace because of the lack of interest and stuborn positioning coming from ingrained beliefs about the value of plant genetic resources.

- Developing countries want to keep tight control over biodiversity resources either because they believe there is a lot of money to be made out of those resources or because they want to pre-

---

45 *See* Report of the Commission on Genetic Resources for Food and Agriculture, Sixth Extraordinary Session, June 25–30, 2001, CGRFA-Ex 6/01/REP.

46 *Id.*

47 Art. 13(d).

48 Art. 4.

vent others from benefiting from those resources. But as a commentator put it: "keeping yams off the Undertaking in the hope that Yam.com will make the NASDAQ or for the sake of retribution (to keep others from rampant yam patenting)" will eventually jeopardize food security;[49]

- The North assumes that the best germplasm is already duplicated in its national gene banks. The South may still contain valuable material, but the interest of the North in such material is low. Many companies believe that biotechnology will achieve more by rearranging the genetic material in the already found seeds than what would be achieved by bioprospecting. In addition, since the South does not have many national gene banks, it benefits most from the biodiversity resources located in the IARCs,[50] making the Undertaking an issue of relatively little importance to the North.

Eventually an agreement was reached on November 2001. The agreement does not differ substantially from the negotiating text of July.[51] The agreement aims to establish "an efficient, effective and transparent" multilateral system to facilitate access to germplasm for the purposes of food and agriculture,[52] and to share "in a fair and equitable way" the benefits from the utilization of resources.[53] The facilitated access provided by the agreement will be accomplished through a standard Material Transfer Agreement (MTA), the provisions of which are to be adopted by the Governing Body.[54] It is clarified also that:

---

49 "Frequently Unasked Questions about the International Undertaking on Plant Genetic Resources," *RAFI Communiqué*, April 18, 2001, available online at *http:// www.rafi.org*.

50 *Id.*

51 *See supra* note 45.

52 Art. 12.3(a). The treaty does not address "chemical, pharmaceutical and/or other non-food/feed industrial uses."

53 Art. 10.2.

54 Art. 12.4 (the Governing Body of the Treaty is composed by all Contracting Parties). *See* Arts. 19.1 and 19.2 (all decisions of the Governing Body shall be taken by consensus unless by consensus another method of arriving at a decision on certain measures is reached).

- access shall be granted expeditiously and free of charge;[55]
- recipients must not claim intellectual property rights on the plant genetic resources or their components "in the form received from the Multilateral System" (implying that modification, isolation, or purification could be subject to intellectual property rights);[56]
- access to genetic resources protected by intellectual property rights will be subject to national regulation consistent with the relevant international agreements;[57] and
- access to resources found *in situ* should be subject to national legislation and, in the absence of such legislation, to standards set by the Governing Body established under the treaty.

The treaty clearly covers the resources held in the *ex situ* collections of the International Agricultural Research Centers and other international institutions[58] and invites all other holders of plant genetic resources to include their resources in the Multilateral System.[59] The Governing Body reserves the right to take action—in terms of continuing to allow access to the system resources—against the legal and natural persons that fail to include their resources within the system.[60]

Facilitated access is pre-conditioned on the equitable sharing of benefits. Such benefits may include exchange of information,[61] access to and transfer of technology,[62] and capacity building.[63] The most contentious issue during the negotiations was that of sharing the benefits from the commercialization of germplasm resources. The treaty pro-

55 Art. 12.3(b).

56 Art. 12.3(d).

57 Art. 12.3(f).

58 Art. 11.5.

59 Arts. 11.2 and 11.3.

60 Art. 11.4.

61 Art. 13.2(a).

62 Art. 13.2(b).

63 Art. 13.2(c).

vides that the recipient of a product must pay to a Trust Account[64] an equitable share of the benefits arising from the commercialization of the product.[65] Such sharing is only voluntary in the case the product is still available without restriction to others for further research and breeding.[66] The Governing Body must decide in its first meeting the "level, form and manner of payment" in accordance with commercial practice.[67] The benefits from these payments must flow to the farmers of all countries, including the farmers of developing countries and countries with economies in transition.[68]

The treaty covers farmers' rights leaving their protection up to national law.[69] The treaty emphasizes the importance of the Global Plan of Action[70] and the *ex situ* collections of the International Agricultural Research Centers.[71] In this respect, the treaty calls for the development of international plant genetic resources networks[72] and for a global information system on plant genetic resources for food and agriculture.[73]

An issue that remained contentious until the final round of negotiations involved the Annex to the convention that covers the list of crops that are subject to the Multilateral System. Developing countries, assuming that bilateral contracts would be more financially rewarding, succeeded in keeping many important crops and forages off the Annex. The

---

64 Art. 13.3(f).

65 Art. 13.2(d).

66 Art. 13.2(d)(ii) (however, the Governing Body may decide to make such contributions mandatory, even when the product is still available to others for research and breeding).

67 *Id.* (the Governing Body may decide to exempt from such payments small farmers in developing countries and in countries with economies in transition).

68 Art. 13.3.

69 Art. 9.

70 Art. 14.

71 Art. 15.

72 Art. 16.

73 Art. 17.

convention covers 35 crops and 29 forages out of 100 food crops and 18,000 forages important for food security. Food crops such as soya, sugar cane, oil palm and groundnut are missing from the Annex.[74] This omission is bound to create uncertainty about the proper means of access to those resources given that such resources are already located in the International Agricultural Research Centers and national gene banks.

Another issue that caused heated debate was that of a potential assertion of intellectual property rights over germplasm resources. The compromise provision provides that intellectual property rights cannot be declared on plant genetic resources for food and agriculture and their genetic parts or components "in the form received by the Multilateral System."[75] This means that modified resources, by bio-engineering and breeding, could be patented shifting the burden of proof to the patent system to determine whether a modification is innovative enough to qualify for protection. The provision, though, still does not clarify whether derived material such as varieties, genes and gene sequences can be patented.[76] A related proposal that subordinated the treaty to the TRIPs agreement[77]—as a means for guaranteeing the protection of intellectual property rights—was not eventually adopted. It was decided, instead, to include in the Preamble a provision that recited that all international agreements should be mutually supportive and that there must not be "a hierarchy between this treaty and other international agreements."

The treaty was adopted with 116 votes in favor, zero against and two abstentions by the United States and Japan. Both countries cited concerns about the breadth of the protection of intellectual property rights under the treaty.

---

74 P. Mulvany, "Global Seed Treaty Hangs in the Balance," 46 *Biotechnology and Development Monitor* 20 (2001).

75 Art. 12.3(d).

76 The United States had supported a proposal according to which Article 13 was modified to clearly specify that any derived material could be patented. *See* Mulvany, *supra* note 74.

77 *See supra* note 23.

## 1.4. Property Rights over Indigenous Peoples' Knowledge and Farmers' Rights

*The Protection of Indigenous Peoples' Knowledge*

Given the protection of intellectual property rights over bio-engineered living organisms, developing countries have claimed that in both biodiversity and biotechnology, the final product of legal protection is a living organism. If developed countries can grant intellectual property rights over genes, developing countries should be able to grant property rights over resources that would have disappeared without the input of indigenous peoples and farmers. In this respect the Biodiversity Convention provides that the knowledge, innovations and practices of indigenous and local communities can be used only with the approval of those communities and the benefits from the use must be equitably shared.[78]

Since intellectual property rights over natural resources cannot be enforced, it has been proposed that a system of *sui generis* rights must be established. Such rights, under the name "traditional resource rights," it is proposed, would constitute a framework into which the claims of indigenous groups could be integrated.[79] Such rights could be established for all resources *in situ* and *ex situ* that have been experimented with and have been singled out for use by indigenous peoples.

*Farmers' Rights*

The 1989 version of the Undertaking on Plant Genetic Resources recognized, in both Annexes I and II, farmers' rights[80] which are "vested in the international community, as a trustee for present and future generations of farmers," so as to ensure full benefits to farmers and support for their contributions.[81] The International Treaty on Plant Genetic

78 *See supra* note 29.

79 Darrell A. Posey, "Intellectual Property Rights and Just Compensation for Indigenous Peoples," 6 *Anthropology Today* 13 (1990).

80 According to FAO Resolution 4/89, farmers' rights involve rights arising from the past, present, and future contributions of farmers to conservation and improvement of plant genetic resources. *See supra* note 44.

81 *Id.*

Resources also clearly recognizes the rights of farmers[82] but leaves it up to national law to determine the breadth of those rights.[83]

A variety of mechanisms have been proposed for the protection of farmers' rights ranging from an international fund to market mechanisms or a mixture of mechanisms.[84]

The implementation of such mechanisms, though, could encounter problems:[85]

- Landraces present more variety in their gene pool than breeder varieties that are uniform and stable. Genetic techniques to identify landraces could be costly and inconclusive.
- It would be difficult to identify the farmers to be compensated. There is no global institutional mechanism that represents the interests of farmers. Therefore either an international association of farmers must be established or states could represent the interests of farmers. But again which farmers of which states must be compensated will become an issue.
- The basis for the contributions to a fund that will compensate farmers could create significant conflict.[86]

As mentioned above, a mechanism was eventually adopted under the Treaty on Plant Genetic Resources for Food and Agriculture according

---

82 Article 9.1 provides that "[c]ontracting Parties recognize the enormous contributions that the local and indigenous communities and farmers of all regions of the world . . . have made and will continue to make for the conservation and development of plant genetic resources which constitute the basis of food and agriculture production throughout the world."

83 Art. 9.2.

84 Commission on Plant Genetic Resources, Sixth Session, Item 8 of the Provisional Agenda, Revision of the International Undertaking on Plant Genetic Resources, Analysis of Some Technical, Economic and Legal Aspects for Consideration in Stage II: Access to Plant Genetic Resources and Farmers' Rights, June 19–30, 1995, CPGR-6/95/8 Supp. (CPGR-EX1/94/5 SUPP.).

85 *Id.*

86 It has been proposed that contributions could be based on the sales of improved varieties, the value added in agriculture, the gross domestic product or the scale of a country's contributions to the FAO or the UN. *Id.* at 54.

to which companies must make payments to a Trust Account every time a patent removes germplasm from the public domain.[87] This provision imposes, for the first time, a tax on companies that use and experiment with germplasm when such experimentation is fruitful. Many issues, though, remain unresolved such as the level, form and manner of payment. The Governing Body established under the treaty will eventually decide how the payments will be structured and may decide to establish "different levels of payment for various categories of recipients."[88]

## 2. THE IARCS AS GATEKEEPERS OF PLANT GENETIC RESOURCES

### 2.1. The Establishment and Evolution of the IARCs

The Consultative Group on International Agricultural Research (CGIAR) was established in 1971,[89] as an informal group of private and public donors and it is supporting 18 IARCs. The CGIAR is co-sponsored jointly by the FAO, the United Nations Development Program (UNDP), the UNEP and the World Bank. The CGIAR is not a formal legal entity; it works because of the consensus of its member-donors.[90] The establishing principle of the CGIAR is decentralization and networking.[91] The last thing that member-donors wanted, when they put together the

87 *See supra* notes 64 and 65.

88 Art. 13(2)(d).

89 Before the birth of the CGIAR in 1971, the Ford and the Rockefeller foundations established four international agricultural research centers: the International Rice Research Institute (IRRI), the Center for the Improvement of Maize and Wheat (CIMMYT), the International Institute for Tropical Agriculture (IITA), and the International Center for Tropical Agriculture (CIAT). These institutions helped to create optimism about the future of the world food. Except for serving as gene banks, these institutions are involved in breeding high-yield rice and wheat varieties. *See* M.S. Swaminathan, "Seeds and Property Rights: A View from the CGIAR System," in *Seeds and Sovereignty, supra* note 2, at 231, 232.

90 A statement of the CGIAR organizational structure, objective and composition was adopted in the first meeting of the Group. *See* Warren C. Baum, *Partners Against Hunger: The Consultative Group on International Agricultural Research* 107 (World Bank ed., 1986).

91 Juma, *supra* note 1, at 89.

CGIAR, was for it to become another bureaucratic international institution. The CGIAR's lack of legal personality and the IARCs' lack of international legal personality have undermined the international mission of the CGIAR system. The movement for the nationalization of genetic resources including resources located in the IARCs has increased efforts to strengthen the international legal personality of the IARCs.

The CGIAR started with four Centers—the CIAT, the CIMMYT, the IITA, and the IIRI that had already been established as nonprofit institutions by the Rockefeller and the Ford foundations—in Colombia, Mexico, Nigeria, and Philippines, respectively. Today the number of Centers has increased to 18, and the voluntary contributions that sustain them are about 300 million annually.[92] The Centers operate from year to year because their funding is determined on an annual basis. Often funding is difficult to ensure and the Centers have to shrink their operations.[93] Since funding comes from voluntary donors,[94] center/

---

92 Selcuk Ozgediz, *Governance and Management of the CGIAR Centers* 139 (CGIAR Study Paper Number 27, World Bank ed., 1991) [hereinafter CGIAR Governance].

93 *See CGIAR Mid-Term Meeting: Summary of Proceedings and Decisions,* 1994 [hereinafter 1994 Meeting].

94 The CGIAR membership includes the following countries: Australia, Austria, Bangladesh, Brazil, Canada, China, Colombia, Côte d' Ivoire, Denmark, Egypt, Finland, France, Germany, India, Indonesia, Iran, Ireland, Italy, Japan, Kenya, Korea, Luxembourg, Mexico, the Netherlands, Nigeria, Norway, Pakistan, the Philippines, Romania, Russia, Spain, Sweden, Switzerland, Syria, the United Kingdom, and the Unites States.

Membership includes also foundations—the Ford Foundation, the International Development Research Center, the Kellogg Foundation, and the Rockefeller Foundation; international and regional organizations—the African Development Bank, the Arab Fund for Economic and Social Development, the Asian Development Bank, the European Commission, the FAO, the Inter-American Development Bank, the International Fund for Agricultural Development, the OPEC Fund for International Development, the United Nations Development Program; the United Nations Environment Program and the World Bank.

Over the last two years the CGIAR has lost 20 percent of its funding. *See* Kunda Dixit, "Asia-Agriculture: Green Revolution to Gene Revolution," *Inter Press Service*, Nov. 1, 1995.

donor relationships are extremely important.[95] In general, the CGIAR system has worked well and the Centers' relationships with their host countries have been good.[96] As mentioned before, the Centers have played a crucial role in the preservation of food and agricultural resources. Well over 100,000 samples of materials held in the CGIAR collections were distributed in 1990 for use worldwide.[97]

The Centers characterize themselves as independent and autonomous nonprofit organizations of an international status. A more accurate description for most Centers until recently was that of nonprofit institutions with an international mission. Still many Centers do not have an international legal personality. Only some Centers have established firmly their international character. The nonprofit character of the Centers has to do with the administrative structure of the Centers which resembles more that of a nonprofit corporation rather than that of an international organization. The Centers are administered by a board of trustees[98] and a director. The director is the decision-maker at the Centers.[99] The Technical Advisory Committee (TAC) of the

---

95 CGIAR Governance, *supra* note 92, at 7.

96 *Id.* at xx.

97 *Diversity for Development: The Strategy of the International Plant Genetic Resources Institute* 16 (IPGRI ed., 1993) [hereinafter IPGRI Strategy].

98 For a description of who can be elected on the board of trustees, *see CGIAR Newsletter*, May 1996.

99 The initial boards were modeled after the boards of the Rockefeller and the Ford Foundations. After the CGIAR took over in 1971, members of the boards were replaced by CGIAR nominees who serve on a personal basis. The boards of the CGIAR Centers resemble corporate boards rather than boards of nonprofit institutions because they are small and have high attendance rates. However, the boards do not direct like corporate boards. The Centers are director-led rather than board-led. The director is the most powerful person at the Centers. The director is the person who prepares the policy and strategy of the Centers. The boards basically oversee the policymaking of the director. The boards of the IARCs have been subjected to criticism for lacking accountability for the Centers' performance and for being too much influenced by donors and host countries. *See* CGIAR Governance, *supra* note 92, at 16, 17, 25. The desire to keep on the boards nationals of major donors does not necessarily mean that the candidates selected are the most responsive to the Centers' needs. *Id.* at 21.

CGIAR[100] makes recommendations on research programs and priorities, monitors performance through program and budget reviews, and supervises the external reviews[101] of the Centers.[102]

Individual donors allocate their contributions to the Center of their choice. The World Bank contributes the difference between the approved budgets and the collective donor contributions.[103] The governance system of the Centers is based on trust and confidence. The CGIAR decisions are not binding on individual Centers since the CGIAR has no formal legal personality and the Centers are independent and autonomous.[104]

Some Centers such as the CIMMYT, the IRRI, and the International Potato Center (CIP) focus on one commodity for which they have a global mandate. Other Centers have a regional or a global mandate for more than one commodity, for example, the International Center for Tropical Agriculture (CIAT), the International Center for Agricultural Research in Dry Areas (ICARDA), the International Institute for Tropical Agriculture (IITA), the West Africa Rice Development Organization (WARDA), the International Crops Research Institute for the Semi-Arid Tropics (ICRISAT) and the International Livestock Research Institute (ILRI). Other Centers perform specialized functions in food policy

---

100 The TAC is comprised by a chairperson and 18 scientists drawn equally from developed and developing countries.

101 In order to compensate for the lack of accountability of the Centers, the CGIAR has initiated External Management Reviews (ERMs). These periodic reviews are the only way for the CGIAR to receive information about the performance of the Centers. Also donors express their discontent with the Centers by withdrawing funding. *See* CGIAR Governance, *supra* note 92, at 25.

102 *See* Warren C. Baum, *Partners Against Hunger: The Consultative Group on International Agricultural Research* (World Bank ed., 1986). The CGIAR is served also by a Secretariat provided by the World Bank and based in Washington DC. The Secretariat reports to the CGIAR chairperson, a vice president of the World Bank designated by the Bank's president after consultation with the CGIAR members. The Secretariat coordinates fund-raising among donor members, provides administrative services, and keeps donors informed about the scientific programs and finances of the Centers. *Id.* at 140.

103 *Id.*

104 *Id.* at 25.

research—the International Food Policy Research Institute (IFPRI) and the International Service for National Agricultural Research (ISNAR). In recent years the CGIAR has sponsored Centers that work in the area of agroforestry and forestry such as the International Center for Research in Agroforestry based in Kenya (ICRAF) and the Center for International Forestry Research based in Indonesia (CIFOR).[105] These Centers focus on the conservation and management of biodiversity in tropical forests. The CIFOR seeks to develop novel approaches for the management and preservation of existing forests. The efforts of the CIFOR are based on a realistic agenda. The CIFOR does not seek to protect all tropical forests. This would be infeasible because a growing population will force the conversion of many forests into agricultural fields and human settlements. The CIFOR's mandate is to ensure that only land suitable for agriculture is converted and that the richest in diversity forests are adequately protected.[106]

The International Plant Genetic Resources Institute (IPGRI), formerly known as International Board of Plant Genetic Resources (IBPGR), is one of the most significant policymaking Centers. The IBPGR was established in 1974, when the loss of valuable landraces became so widespread that it was recognized that an international network of gene banks was indispensable. In the first years of its life the IBPGR was involved in collecting germplasm from all around the world and depositing it in gene banks. It also assisted in gene bank development in the third world.[107] Today the principal objective of the IPGRI is to assist the

---

105 Except for the Centers affiliated with the CGIAR, there are other regional Centers such as the Centro Agronomico Tropical de Investigacion y Ensenanza based in Costa Rica (CATIE) and the Asian Vegetable Research and Development Center based in Taiwan (AVRDC).

106 "Poor Farmers Could Destroy Half of the Remaining Tropical Forest," *CGIAR Forestry Press Release*, Aug. 5, 1996, available online at *http://www. world-bank.org/html/cgiar/press/forest.html*.

107 In the first decade of its life the IPGRI focused on collecting threatened germplasm and facilitating long-term conservation in the base collections maintained by 40 international and national gene banks. By the year 1991, almost 200,000 samples had been collected by missions sponsored by the IBPGR. An important contribution of the IPGRI is the introduction of a standardized system for characterizing germplasm. This system has been adopted by institutions all over the world. *See* IPGRI Strategy, *supra* note 97, at 6.

national[108] and regional programs of developing countries. Another objective is to build crop and regional networks.[109] The IPGRI has been transformed from an organization heavily involved in plant collection to an organization playing a supportive role in national and regional programs.

A consensus seems to be developing today that national programs constitute the core of international efforts to save genetic resources.[110] Actually the whole orientation of the IARCs seems to have changed since their inception. The purpose of the CGIAR to increase the production of food worldwide[111] has been amended to stress partnership with national programs.[112] It is increasingly felt that the "more food" rationale for continued agricultural research is simplistic and anachronistic and that if the CGIAR is to command the support of the international community additional emphasis should be placed on the alleviation of poverty and hunger.[113] The 1995 Lucerne Declaration and Action Program adopted at the CGIAR Ministerial-Level Meeting firmly established that the renewed purpose of the CGIAR is "to combat poverty and hunger in the world by mobilizing both indigenous knowledge and modern science" with a greater emphasis on North-South cooperation.[114]

---

108 National programs include: The Central Research Institute for Food Crops in Bogor, Indonesia which preserves mostly rice varieties. The Vavilov institute in Russia, the NSSL in the United States, the Instituto del Germoplasma in Italy, the Plant Germplasm Institute at the University of Kyoto, Japan. There are also maize institutes in Portugal and in Mexico (the Mexican National Program (INIA)). *See* Donald L. Plucknett et al., *Gene Banks and the World's Food* 119–40 (1987).

109 One such successful network was established in Europe, the European Cooperative Program for Crop Genetic Resources Networks (ECP/GR), and has stimulated the development of 22 European crop databases. *See* IPGRI Strategy, *supra* note 97, at 7.

110 *Id.* at 13.

111 Increase of agricultural production was not only a goal but also a value held by the Centers. *See* CGIAR Governance, *supra* note 92, at 10–11.

112 IPGRI Strategy, *supra* note 97, at 15.

113 1994 Meeting, *supra* note 93.

114 CGIAR Ministerial-Level Meeting, Lucerne, Switzerland, Feb. 9–10, 1995, available online at *http://www.worldbank.org/html/cgiar/publications/declara.html*.

Developing countries have viewed the IARCs as institutions created to strengthen the agricultural superiority of the North. The clientele relationship between the donors—who frequently are developed countries—and the Centers has assisted in perpetuating such perceptions. The Lucerne Action program, therefore, specifically provides that the CGIAR must broaden its membership to include more developing countries and must increasingly participate in the National Agricultural Research Systems (NARS)[115] of developing countries. The agricultural research institutions of the host countries have gradually become important clients of the Centers located in those countries. The majority of the ICRISAT's activities in India are in conformity with the needs of Indian research institutions. The IRRI has filled also most of the needs for a national program in the Philippines.[116] However, the donor/clientele relationship is still strong and the Centers need to complete the transition "from a donor/client approach to equal partnership of all participants from the South and North within the CGIAR system."[117] But the desire to increase the participation of the South should not become so prevalent as to detract from the international mission of the Centers. Agricultural programs in Eastern Europe may need the support and expertise of the CGIAR and should not just be relegated to secondary status.[118]

Also the Centers aim to become more open and to encourage participation in their activities of private and non-governmental organizations. Today private companies are not significant clients of the Centers. But this is expected to change in the future.[119] It is increasingly realized that

---

115 Public sector agricultural research is particularly important in developing countries. In most developing countries there is not much private agricultural research activity and national agro-industries are in their infancy. Most agricultural products are sold to developing countries by transnational corporations. *See* "Why Is Public Agricultural Research Needed?" *CGIAR Newsletter*, May 1996.

116 CGIAR Governance, *supra* note 92, at 91.

117 *See* Lucerne Action Plan, CGIAR Ministerial-Level Meeting Feb 9–10, 1995, available online at *http://www.worldbank.org/html/cgiar/publications/declara.html*. The goals of the Lucerne Declaration and Lucerne Action Plan were reaffirmed in the 1996 CGIAR Mid-Term Meeting.

118 According to the Lucerne Action Plan, research in Eastern Europe is to be undertaken only if separate and additional funding is secured. *See id.*

119 CGIAR Governance, *supra* note 92, at 89.

more centralization and coordination is needed in the Centers activities. While the CGIAR is committed to "creating a system-wide program on genetic resources," it is still far from becoming an organization that deals in a systematic fashion with genetic resources. Systematization and centralization, it is generally agreed, should not be pursued to the point of eradicating the informal character of the Centers.[120]

The Committee of Board Chairs (CBC) and the Center Directors Committee (CDC) of the CGIAR have recently recommended the creation of a federation of Centers and an action plan for the immediate steps to improve inter-Center collaboration.[121] The federation consisting of a coordinator (called "federation office") and each individual center as a separate legal entity has been proposed as the best organizational structure to deal with the challenging mission of the centers. The vision, goal and mission of the CGIAR, emphasized in the 2000 Mid-Term Meeting, are to reduce poverty in developing countries.[122] Other recommendations for the better functioning of the Centers include the creation of an Executive Council, the transformation of TAC into a Science Council and the creation of a System Office for integrated communication strategy and fund raising.[123]

---

120 1994 Meeting, *supra* note 93. During the 1994 Meeting it was decided that a fifteen-member Steering Committee must be established in order to coordinate the activities of the Centers. However, proposals for a "single board" for all the Centers and the division of the Centers' programs into system-wide and regional activities was rejected. According to the Lucerne Action Plan: "[c]ollegiality and informality are important and durable assets of the CGIAR. Therefore, the CGIAR should not be established as a formal international organization, but could benefit from strengthening its decision making processes and consultative mechanisms." *See* Lucerne Action Plan, *supra* note 117.

121 Charting the CGIAR's Future—Reshaping the CGIAR Organization, Oct. 19, 2001, ICW/00/07-7 (CBC/CDC Report on Governance, Structure and Management).

122 Draft Interim Executive Council Recommendations on CGIAR Reform, Oct. 15, 2001, AGM/01/04 (An Integrated Proposal for the Annual General Meeting 2001).

123 *Id.*

## 2.2. The Legal Personality of the IARCs

The Centers' legal personality has acquired importance since, after the adoption of the Biodiversity Convention, there have been increasing demands for the repatriation of genetic material located at the Centers.

The legal personality of the Centers is ambiguous, a breed between a national organization and an international organization. The four pioneer Centers were created by an agreement between the host government and individual donors and not by a treaty between states, the formal way of institution-making in international law. However, the constitutional character of the Centers has evolved and some of the Centers have successfully stabilized their international personality. In 1992 the IBPGI was renamed IPGRI, and the agreement that transformed the legal personality of the Center was signed by states making, thus, the IPGRI an international institution.[124] The international legal personality of the IRRI has also been recognized explicitly in an agreement signed by states "recognizing the international legal personality of the International Rice Research Institute."[125]

While some Centers have kept their status as nonprofit institutions, others have reformed their constitutions, which are now appended to agreements signed by international institutions that play the role of the founding institutions of the Centers. The CIMMYT constitution was initially appended to an agreement signed by Mexico and the Rockefeller foundation; but it is now based on an agreement between the World Bank and the UNDP.[126] A similar arrangement governs the legal status of the CIAT.[127] While agreements between international organizations

---

124 *See* Agreement on the Establishment of the International Plant Genetic Resources Institute, Oct. 9, 1992.

125 *See* Agreement Recognizing the International Legal Personality of the International Rice Research Institute, May 19, 1995.

126 Agreement between the International Bank for Reconstruction and Development and the United Nations Development Program on the Establishment of the Centro Internacional de Mejoramiento de Maiz y Trigo, April 29, 1988.

127 Agreement between the International Bank for Reconstruction and Development and the United Nations Development Program on the Establishment of the Centro Internacional de Agricultura Tropical, May 28, 1986.

to establish a third organization are not widely encountered in international law, the explicit treaty-making ability of the World Bank and the implicit treaty-making ability of the UNDP should render the international legal personality of the CIMMYT and the CIAT indubitable.[128]

The CIP's constitution is still based on a decree of the Peruvian government and an agreement of scientific cooperation between the government of Peru and the North Carolina State University in the United States.[129] The constitution of the CIP does not even mention that the Center is an institution of an international character. However, the agreement between the North Carolina State University and the Peruvian government clearly provides that by the establishment of the CIP the potato programs of all countries in the world will be able "to use to a maximum the germplasm that exists in Peru, in Andean countries and other areas of the world."[130]

The IITA is based on a decree of the Nigerian government. And, while the nonprofit and autonomous character of the Center is mentioned, there is no mention of an international character.[131] Actually the

---

[128] An international organization may have treaty-making powers if such powers are explicitly or implicitly mentioned in its constitution. While the constitution of the World Bank explicitly confers to the Bank treaty-making power, the same is not true with the UNDP. The treaty-making power of the UNDP can be inferred from the extensive powers that have been granted to the UNDP in its constitutive instrument, the General Assembly Resolution that established the UNDP and General Assembly Resolutions that subsequently strengthened the role of the UNDP. However, since the treaty-making power of the UNDP is not explicit in its constitutive instrument, it can still be challenged. *See, e.g.*, GA Res. 2688 (XXV), Dec. 11, 1970.

For the treaty-making power of international organizations, *see generally* Ian Brownlie, *Principles of Public International Law* 683–84 (1990). *See also* D.W. Bowett, *The Law of International Institutions* 304–08 (1975); Chris N. Okeke, *Controversial Subjects of Contemporary International Law: An Examination of the New Entities in International Law and their Treaty Making Capacity* 193–94 (1974).

[129] The Scientific Cooperation Agreement between Peru and the North Carolina University has been approved by Decree Law No. 20025, May 23, 1973. *See* also Supreme Decree No. 240-68-AG which approved the by-laws of the CIP.

[130] Preamble (d).

[131] Decree No. 32—International Institute of Tropical Agriculture.

Center has yet to formalize its affiliation with the CGIAR. Other Centers are still based on contracts between private foundations and host governments. The ICRISAT was created in 1972 by an agreement between the Ford Foundation acting on behalf of the CGIAR and the Indian Government, and it is still based on the same agreement.[132]

The establishment of the ICARDA is based on a unique arrangement. An agreement between Syria and the International Development Research Center (IDRC), a Canadian agency acting as an Executive Agency for the CGIAR, established the Center, whose Charter was eventually signed by the World Bank, the UNDP and the FAO. The bilateral agreement between the IDRC and Syria and the signature of the ICARDA charter by three international institutions certainly establishes the ICARDA as more than a national institution.[133]

A question that requires investigation, because it is related with the ownership issue, is the future of germplasm in case the Centers are dissolved. According to the CIMMYT constitution, if the CIMMYT is dissolved, its assets will be retained by the host country or other collaborating countries after an agreement between the governments of those countries and the Board of the CIMMYT in consultation with the CGIAR.[134] Similar provisions are included in the IPGRI, the ICARDA, and the CIP constitutions.[135] However, dissolution is not automatic and

---

132 Constitution of International Crops Research Institute for the Semi-Arid Tropics (ICRISAT), July 5, 1972.

133 Agreement between the Government of Syrian Arabic Republic and the International Development Research Center acting as an Executive Agency on behalf of the CGIAR for the establishment of the International Center for Agricultural Research in the Dry Areas (ICARDA), June 28, 1976.

134 Article 14 of the Constitution of Centro Internacional de Mejoramiento de Maiz y Trigo:

> In case of dissolution, the assets of CIMMYT, situated in the host country or other collaborating countries *shall be retained by such countries* and used for similar purposes, or distributed to institutions having purposes similar to CIMMYT *in the respective countries* after agreement between the governments of these countries and the Board in consultation with the members of the CGIAR [emphasis added].

135 The dissolution provisions of the CIP are located in the ninth Clause of the

does not depend on the will of the host country. Dissolution is generally subject to the approval of a Center's board. Members of the Board are mostly donors. And the host country, which is to gain most from the dissolution, may not have a significant say in the dissolution of the Centers.

Still, the dissolution provisions undermine the international character of the Centers, since their assets are not to be inherited by an international organization but by national governments. The dissolution provisions need to be amended in order to grant the FAO or another international institution the authority to decide the future of the assets of the Centers.

The establishing documents of other Centers do not even provide for the fate of genetic resources after dissolution. For instance, the Nigerian decree establishing the ITTA explicitly provides that upon the termination of the ITTA all physical plant and equipment shall become the property of the Nigerian government. No explicit provision is included, though, on the disposition of germplasm resources.[136]

Other constitutions have addressed the issue of the future of germplasm resources after dissolution. For instance, the IRRI charter provides that in case the Institute is terminated all physical plant, equipment, and other assets will become the property of the University of Philippines with the "the exception of such funds and other assets, *like the Institute's gene bank and genetic resources*, that shall have been assigned in trust to the Institute for others or donated to the Institute, and shall have been made subject to some other conditions in respect to their disposition upon dissolution of the Institute [emphasis added]."[137] It would have bolstered the international character of the IRRI, if an international institution, like the FAO, were to become the caretaker of all germplasm resources and were to decide their future disposition.

---

Agreement for Scientific Cooperation Between the Government of Peru and the North Carolina State University.

136 Art. 14, Decree No. 32.

137 Art. XV, Section 2, Charter of the International Rice Research Institute.

The WARDA does not share the general structure of other IARCs. The WARDA has been established as a regional association. Membership in the association is restricted to the African States of the West African Region. The WARDA constitution provides that if the association is terminated, measures must be taken for the proportionate distribution of the assets of the association among Member States, with the exception of installations, equipment, and material owned by the Association which "shall, as far as possible continue to be used for the purpose of which they had originally been acquired." The WARDA constitution provides explicitly that "[i]nstallations, equipment and material made available to the Association by Cooperating States and Organizations shall be disposed of in consultation with the States and Organizations concerned." This provision ensures that germplasm which could be traced back to the countries of origin could be returned to those countries, if those countries so request. It is clarified, therefore, that germplasm coming from other countries and regions is not material upon which the association has ownership.

Only the dissolution provisions of the ICRISAT seem to give the CGIAR a greater margin of discretion about the future of germplasm resources after dissolution. The constitution provides that "[o]n dissolution the disposition of all other assets [except for land and fixed capital improvements] shall be determined by the Consultative Group on International Agricultural Research after receiving recommendations from the Governing Board, such disposition to be to organizations which are formed and operated exclusively for scientific and educational purposes."[138] The constitution of the International Service for National Agricultural Research (ISNAR) grants to the members of the CGIAR significant discretion on what to do with the ISNAR's assets.[139] However, the ISNAR is not a gene bank. Its goal is to strengthen the agricultural research capabilities of developing countries.[140] Another research institute, the International Food and Policy Research Institute

---

138 Art. XII, Section 2, ICRISAT Constitution.

139 Chapter XIII, ISNAR Constitution.

140 Art. III, ISNAR Constitution.

authorizes a domestic court (the United States District Court of the District of Columbia) to decide which organizations will get the IFPRI assets.[141]

## 2.3. The Status of the IARCs' Germplasm Collections

In 1994, twelve IARCs signed agreements to place their gene bank resources under the auspices of the FAO.[142] Under the agreements,[143] the Centers remain trustees of the collections for the benefit of the international community and particularly of developing countries.[144] The Centers are placed under the auspices of the FAO as part of a network of gene banks.[145] Under Article 9 of the agreements, the Centers are under an obligation to provide germplasm and related information directly to users *without restriction* through the FAO, for the purposes of scientific research, plant breeding or genetic resource conservation. While the term "without restriction" could be interpreted to mean that resources are freely available, this is not the case. In a joint statement the FAO and the CGIAR[146] specified that "*without restriction*" should be interpreted in accordance with the Convention on Biological Diversity and should not be understood in any way as affecting the rights of countries under the convention. Article 9 is also subject to Article 10,

---

141 Sixth Article of Incorporation of the International Food Policy Research Institute.

142 The Centers that are now under the auspices of the FAO are: the CIAT, the CIMMYT, the CIP, the ICARDA, the International Center for Research in Agroforestry (ICRAF), the ICRISAT, the IITA, the International Livestock Center for Africa (ILCA), the IPGRI, the International Network for the Improvement of Banana and Plantain (INIBAP), the IRRI, the WARDA and the CIFOR.

143 Twelve agreements were signed between each individual Center and the FAO. The agreements were signed by the CGIAR chairman and the FAO director.

144 Art. 3, Commission on Plant Genetic Resources, First Extraordinary Session, The International Network of Ex Situ Germplasm Collections, Nov.1, 1994, CPGR-Ex1/94/Inf.5/Add .1 [hereinafter Agreement].

145 Art. 2, *id.*

146 Joint Statement of the FAO and the CGIAR Centers on the Agreement Placing CGIAR Germplasm Collections under the Auspices of the FAO, Annex 2, Agreement, *id* [hereinafter Joint Statement].

which provides that the Centers must ensure that any entity that receives germplasm from them is bound by the conditions of Article 3(b). Article 3(b) provides that the Centers shall not claim legal ownership or intellectual property rights over the germplasm contained in their collections or "related information."[147] In other words, anybody who receives germplasm and the Centers themselves cannot assert intellectual property rights over the germplasm. The Joint Statement of the FAO and the CGIAR provides that Article 10 could be satisfied by MTAs that require the recipient not to seek intellectual property rights over the genetic material and to transfer the same obligation to subsequent recipients.[148]

While the Centers and the recipients cannot declare intellectual property rights over the germplasm the same is not true for the country of origin. Article 10 does not "apply to the repatriation of germplasm to the country that provided the germplasm," leaving open the possibility for that country to declare ownership or intellectual property rights over the germplasm.[149] The bottom line is that germplasm can still be transferred, but there are strings attached regarding possible intellectual property rights that may be claimed over it.

The agreements between the IARCs and the FAO may have underlined the international status of the Centers, but the ownership of their collections remains nebulous. Since germplasm is certainly not owned by the FAO and by the International Agricultural Research Centers, the question is whether it is owned by the country of origin. Article 10 does not explicitly provide so, but it certainly suggests so.

It must be noted that the FAO had proposed four types of model agreements (A, B, C, D) for the purpose of securing the international status of the collections located in the International Agricultural Research Centers. Model agreements A and B provided that germplasm collections would be placed under the *jurisdiction* of the FAO, while model agreements C and D provided that the collections would be

---

147 "Related information" refers to information compiled with respect to individual accessions. Such information includes passport, characterization and evaluation data, and information on indigenous knowledge. *Id.*

148 *Id.*

149 Art. 10(b), Agreement, *supra* note 144.

placed under the *auspices* of the FAO. The agreements eventually signed with the IARCs are agreements that place the Centers under the auspices of the FAO. Under-the-auspices agreements are also negotiated with different countries that wish to place their resources under an international umbrella.[150]

Needless to say, an under-the-jurisdiction agreement would have given the FAO more effective control over the IARCs collections, and, potentially, power to decide once and for all the future of the collections. The agreements that place gene banks under the auspices of the FAO implicitly recognize that the FAO is not the owner of the resources. By a process of elimination, since neither the FAO nor the IARCs are the owners, the country of origin must be the owner. An alternative interpretation is that no one has ownership over the pre-convention resources and, thus, the resources belong to the public domain.

It is obvious from the developments that followed the adoption of the FAO/IARCs agreements that the issue that preoccupies countries of origin of germplasm is not ownership *per se*. Asserting ownership over germplasm will amount to nothing more than a blank assertion since most profits from germplasm are not derived just from ownership but from intellectual property rights. Countries are more concerned with ensuring that nobody else asserts property or intellectual property rights over germplasm than asserting their own property rights. The IARCs have to inform formally their clients about their obligation not to claim property or intellectual property rights over germplasm, and their deci-

---

150 Commission on Plant Genetic Resources, Sixth Session, Item 9.2 of the Provisional Agenda, Progress Report on the International Network of Ex Situ Germplasm Collections under the Auspices and/or Jurisdiction of FAO, June 19–30, 1995, CPGR-6/95/12. Thirty-two countries have already indicated their willingness to make their gene banks part of the International Network of the FAO. Collectively these countries hold 46 percent of the world's germplasm accessions. The IPGRI has a register of national and international collections. The register includes a total of about 50 institutions in 18 countries which have agreed to conserve germplasm and make it available to the international community. Recently the IPGRI has agreed that the register should merge with the International Network of the FAO. The International Network then will contain 70 percent of the total accessions. *See* Commission on Plant Genetic Resources, Sixth Session, Item 8 of the Provisional Agenda, Revision of the International Undertaking on Plant Genetic Resources, June 19–30, 1995, CPGR-6/95/8 (CPGR-EX1/94/5), at 10–11.

sion to pass on the same obligation to all future germplasm recipients. From now on, order forms for germplasm located in the IARCs will include a standard provision that germplasm recipients must abstain from claiming ownership or intellectual property rights over germplasm received and that the original recipient must ensure that all successive recipients will not assert any such rights either.[151] Some Centers have gone as far as to challenge patents on germplasm even if that germplasm was not obtained from their own gene banks.[152]

What will happen to the resources located in the International Agricultural Research Centers depends on the implementation of the Treaty on Plant Genetic Resources and the agreements that need to be re-negotiated between the Centers and the FAO. The FAO-CGIAR trust agreements expire in 2002 and they need to be renewed or be replaced with new agreements.

The International Treaty on Plant Genetic Resources has attempted to clarify the role of International Agricultural Centers and the status of their *ex situ* collections. The treaty calls upon the IARCS to sign agreements with the Governing Body of the treaty to ensure that the resources they keep and are listed in Annex I of the treaty are subject to the Multilateral System.[153] All the other resources—not covered by Annex I—will be available under the MTAs that have been signed between the IARCs and the FAO.[154] These MTAs will be amended by the Governing Body so that countries of origin do not have to sign a Material Transfer Agreement for germplasm originating in their territory and that the benefits from the commercialization of germplasm accrue in the Trust Account provided by the treaty.[155] Contracting parties agree to give the

---

[151] Commission on Plant Genetic Resources, Sixth Session, Joint Report by the FAO and the International Plant Genetic Resources Institute (on Behalf of the CGIAR Centers) on the Implementation of the Agreement Signed Between the FAO and the CGIAR Centres on 26 October 1994, June 19–30, 1995, CPGR-6/95/12 ADD.1.

[152] *See supra* note 13.

[153] Art. 15.1(a).

[154] Art. 15.1(b).

[155] *Id.*

IARCs access to their resources provided that these resources are included in Annex I of the treaty. For all other resources collected after the entry into force of the treaty, though, and not covered by the Annex, access can be provided based on bilateral agreements between the country of origin and the IARCs.

## 3. REGULATED FREE ACCESS AS THE OPTIMAL SYSTEM OF ACCESS TO PLANT GENETIC RESOURCES

Countries can gain access to the plant genetic resources of another country by:

- *Free exchange:* the system that prevailed before the 1980s seed wars and led to the establishment of the first gene banks;
- *Bilateral agreements:* the system applied today for access to *in situ* resources;
- *Conforming with the Multilateral System:* the system applied for some resources essential for food and agriculture.

The free access system, as applied before the 1980s, has been marginalized because of the politics involved. The profits made from breeding/bio-engineering have rendered developing countries mindful of the potential of genetic resources that reside within their territory. Developing countries are determined to take advantage of their position as rich-resource countries to gain financial advantages from the North in terms of royalties, capacity building and access to technology.

Bilateral access is today the prevailing mode for transferring germplasm. Access to all *in situ* resources and many resources found in gene banks but not covered by the multilateral treaty are subject to bilateral negotiations between the country of origin and the company/researcher who would like to experiment with the resources. As mentioned before, such agreements entail tremendous transaction costs and have alienated companies from investing in research in the developing world.

The Multilateral System was recently adopted under the Treaty on Plant Genetic Resources for Food and Agriculture. As its name suggests, this system applies only to resources that are used for food and agriculture.

It also covers a limited number of such resources. The system has not been tested yet in practice. The principle it proposes, however, for a multilateral system of access, is quite attractive, especially when compared with bilateral access. A standard document that includes information about the material, the state of origin and the recipient and a standard clause about the rights that could be declared over the material could significantly facilitate the transfer of germplasm in the current environment of distrust.

In the international arena, we can see today elements of all the three systems. Countries with national gene banks can still subscribe to free access if they so wish. The Multilateral System applies only to a certain number of *ex situ* resources for food and agriculture. The rest of the resources could still be free access resources or be subject to bilateral agreements depending on the wishes of the government that controls the resources. For instance, a company fearful of the obligations it may have to undertake under the Multilateral System—in terms of benefit sharing and restrictions on intellectual property rights—could still approach the national laboratories of the United States or other countries, that have not signed the multilateral treaty, to see whether it can get more favorable access. As mentioned before, the same resources that are located in IARCs or are in the hands of developing countries are found often in national gene banks. The success of the Multilateral System depends then on how quickly it will become "universal" in terms of the countries that subscribe to it and how quickly it will become "comprehensive" in terms of the number of resources it covers. A successful Multilateral System for food and agriculture could eventually be expanded to apply to the exchange of *in situ* resources.

Which system is most desirable for the world today depends on the goals states wish to accomplish. If food security is the paramount goal, researchers and companies should be allowed to access and experiment with resources with virtually no controls. If, as some argue, biodiversity is about to disappear in terms of landraces or wild resources, efforts must concentrate on collecting as many species as possible and preserve them in as many gene banks as possible. New methods must be invented also to allow for the *ex situ* preservation of wild species and patent systems must be strengthened to give companies and researchers incentives to collect and experiment with germplasm.

If the goal, on the other hand, is to compensate the farmers of developing countries for their contributions to biodiversity, a bilateral or multilateral system with provisions on benefit sharing and a closer evaluation of the validity of intellectual property rights claims seems to be desirable.

The Multilateral System for food and agricultural resources, established under the Treaty on Plant Genetic Resources, attempts to achieve both goals. To what extent these frequently antithetical goals can be reached simultaneously remains to be seen. A lot will depend on the standardization and clarity the system will bring in international transactions. Given the current state of confusion about the legality and legitimacy of germplasm transfers, the contribution that the Multilateral System could make is to legitimize and facilitate such transfers. In other words, the System could function like other trade regulating systems. The purpose of most international regulations for the trade in goods is the facilitation of trade among countries. As the national barriers to international trade are falling, the purpose of most international trade regulations is to establish clear, uniform and comprehensive standards that would be acceptable to all states and would facilitate commerce. It is hoped that through the establishment of international standards, states will find it more difficult to inhibit trade based on the pretense that their higher national (environmental/safety/labor) standards mandate so.

This study supports a Multilateral Free Access System that functions more as a mechanism that facilitates free access to resources rather than as a mechanism that inhibits such access. It is proposed here that a regulated free access system is preferable to unregulated free access for two reasons:

- Given the politics involved, it is virtually impossible to go back to unregulated free access.
- Without documentation on the chain of transfer of germplasm, it is impossible to establish a mechanism that would ensure that some of the benefits from commercialization trickle down to farmers. Establishing a mechanism to pass on some of the benefits to farmers will address the strong perceptions of inequity and will legitimize the transfer of germplasm.

To accomplish regulated free access, the standards established, under the Multilateral System, must be clear, uniform, and comprehensive:

- A uniform Multilateral System presupposes that the same rules apply to all the resources covered by the system.
- An unambiguous system presupposes that there will be a reasonable level of clarity about the obligations and the rights of the parties affected by the system.
- A comprehensive system entails coverage of all existing useful resources both *in situ* and *ex situ* including but not limited to resources useful for food and agriculture.

The best way to achieve the goals of uniformity and clarity is through a Standard Material Transfer Agreement that would apply to the transfer of all resources. As long as the agreement clearly delineates the rights and obligations of the parties, it could become a successful means for the transfer of genetic resources. The International Treaty on Plant Genetic Resources for Food and Agriculture prescribes for such an agreement but, as mentioned above, given the mandate of the treaty, it will not cover all resources. Also given that the treaty is still considered ambiguous with regard to the intellectual property rights that can be declared over plant genetic resources, more work needs to be accomplished so that the standard agreement is free, as much as possible, of ambiguity.

Overall, it would be ill-advised to abandon the system of intellectual property rights (including breeders' rights and patent rights) over germplasm that has been modified or isolated and can be used commercially due to the human ingenuity. On the other hand, though, traditional knowledge should not be assumed to be free access knowledge.[156] The International Treaty on Plant Genetic Resources has established a mechanism to which corporations will contribute a percentage from the commercialization of genetic resources that have been removed from the public domain. Compensation systems for indigenous' and farmers' knowledge should be explored further to ensure that people receive just compensation for their contributions to the evolution of biodiversity.

---

[156] Traditional healers, for instance, are reluctant to disclose information about the plants they use—clearly signaling that such knowledge is not free access knowledge. Nevertheless, ethnobotanical research has been frequently transcribed from indigenous peoples' practices without their prior consent.

# Conclusion

The international policies for biodiversity protection are based on a series of antinomies:

- *international* instruments that foster *nationalism and bilateralism*;
- *local wildlife management and privatization efforts* undermined by *trade prohibitions and restrictions*;
- general *lack of monitoring and implementation* interspersed by *measures of strict enforcement* that violate basic human rights;
- an *international gene bank system* that stumbles to fulfill its mandate through a maze of *national controls* over germplasm resources.

These antinomies accompanied by an overwhelming lack of urgency and the ensuing lack of funding are evidence that biodiversity protection is of a low priority status in the agenda of many states. States have been disinterested in developing a coherent framework for addressing biodiversity protection issues.

The purpose of this study is to provide such a framework—a framework that is based on what realistically can be achieved *today* by international law in the area of international biodiversity management. As mentioned before, the causes of biodiversity conversion run deep into the conditions of poverty in the developing world. The eradication of these conditions would involve much more than just international environmental lawmaking. It would involve a radical change of many national and international policies in favor of the poor and disenfranchised. Such a radical change does not seem to be forthcoming.

This study, in its attempt to provide a coherent framework for biodiversity protection, takes the conditions of the developing world as a given. Since an improvement of these conditions will not happen overnight, it is proposed that biodiversity protection must be based on three pillars:

- respect for human dignity and human rights—biodiversity protection should not be pursued if it results in human rights violations;
- international biodiversity management through international gene bank management and transnational public or private landscapes; and
- international guidelines for the local management of wildlife supported by the free trade in many of the species considered endangered today.

*Human Rights Standards for International Biodiversity Management*

It is disappointing that even today, with all the awareness about human rights, eco-development efforts proceed despite the protests of local populations who are evicted, deprived of food and basic amenities, and who are even many times tortured or killed.

This study proposes that human rights standards become the minimum basic standards around which biodiversity protection policies develop. Basic human rights such as the right to food and prohibitions against torture and inhumane and degrading punishment should become the center around which biodiversity protection evolves.

It is likely that many states will raise objections against the inclusion of human rights standards in the conservation agenda. Many states view human rights instruments and the scrutiny of their policies by human rights groups as an unnecessary intrusion into their national affairs. States will probably see no reason to expand this scrutiny to biodiversity protection and will resist the inclusion of human rights norms in biodiversity protection instruments. But the absence of human rights norms in biodiversity protection instruments should not discourage human rights organizations from scrutinizing eco-development under a human rights perspective.

*International Biodiversity Management In and Outside Nature*

The second pillar of the framework for biodiversity protection involves the international management of biodiversity resources. International management, as it is understood here, does not involve the creation of an international institution that would manage biodiversity on an international scale. On the contrary, it is proposed that most of biodiversity management should be configured and applied locally.

Some management efforts, however, could benefit from the economies of scale put together by national governments and international institutions. One of them involves gene bank management. Gene bank management is a par excellence international activity. Effective gene bank management involves worldwide efforts to collect and disseminate seeds. A sincere international effort for gene bank development would involve the multiplication of efforts to collect germplasm worldwide, to use it and experiment with it. Gene bank management also involves streamlining many of the existing collections. In order to achieve these desirable results, states need to lower the barriers for access to their resources, to reaffirm the policies for the free exchange of seeds located in international gene banks, and to find innovative ways to compensate indigenous peoples and farmers for their contributions to the evolution of biodiversity.

States also could benefit from the economies of scale of bringing together some areas they wish to protect under regional management networks. Since ecosystems do not know national boundaries, a lot can be achieved in terms of efficiency and effectiveness by private or public efforts to develop regional networks of landscapes. Many such efforts have stumbled, though, because of the economic and political disparities among the countries within the same region.

### *Local Management of Wildlife Supported by Free Trade*

The third pillar on which international management is based is that of local management of resources supported by free trade. The international management of resources does not involve local micro-management. While this study proposes that the international system could provide guidelines for the management of resources, decisions on what to do in particular environments and circumstances should rest with the people who live in the area.

Local management will not be easy, especially since in many countries groups with conflicting interests often claim rights to the same resource. One way effective local management may be achieved is through privatization of wildlife resources. For local management to become successful it must be secured by local institutions that are representative of the population and secure land tenure. Without secure land tenure and strong institutional support local management will fail.

Support for local management does not imply lack of national management (or regional policies in the case of transnational landscapes). It means that national/regional policies must be based on the input of people who are asked to implement them and must be incentive-based rather than rule-oriented. National/regional policies that rely on strict enforcement by violating human rights norms must not be tolerated and must be criticized by human rights and environmental organizations.

The best stimulus that international policymaking can provide for local management is free trade. States must eventually phase out the prohibitions and restrictions included in the CITES Convention and allow for the free trade of products and species that are managed locally. Reestablishing free trade in wildlife will provide the proof that local management systems can succeed and the incentives to protect many of the species that are listed as endangered today.

### *The Role of International Environmental Law*

The Biodiversity Convention is a framework convention that could be interpreted strictly to oppose international biodiversity management. However, as mentioned before, some of the provisions of the convention especially those on restoration, indigenous peoples rights and poverty can be used to plant the seeds of international biodiversity management.

In terms of rhetoric, it is proposed here that future biodiversity protection instruments replace the word "nature reserves" with the term "managed landscapes" or "diverse landscapes." It is proposed also that the terms "conservation" and "preservation" be phased out in favor of "biodiversity management" and "biodiversity protection." Also the words "human rights" and "human dignity" must permeate all instruments on biodiversity protection measures.

In terms of standard setting, human rights standards can be established for biodiversity protection. Human rights standards are monitored vigilantly by human rights groups. These groups can contribute to the enforcement of such rights by affecting a state's reputation. No state wants to be branded a human rights violator.

Gene bank management is also amenable to international standard setting. There is no reason not to standardize globally the procedures applied in gene banks. There is no reason not to establish rules that would unequivocally transform the International Agricultural Research Centers into global institutions. International guidelines can be prescribed also for the management of public or private transnational landscapes.

Overall, local management systems can flourish if they are supported by free trade, international minimum standard setting and national/regional/international guidelines. Overall, biodiversity management would have more chances to succeed if the needs of people who manage biodiversity resources are granted priority in national and international agendas.

# Bibliography

*(Asterisk denotes web site reference.)*


Access to Genetic Resources, 137, 145, 148

Acts, Amendments and Appropriate Authorities: CAMPFIRE's Legal Framework, 80*

Agroecology and In Situ Conservation of Native Crop Diversity in the Developing World (Alteri & Merrick), 93

Aluna: The Place Where the Mother Was Born (Kemf), 55

The Amazon Colonization Program (Jordan, Almeida & Campari, eds.), 51, 72

Amazonian Caboclo Society: An Essay on Invisibility and Peasant Economy (Nugent), 55, 56

An Appropriation of Evolution's Values (Swanson), 45

Are There Alternatives to Destruction (Robinson), 50

Asia Environment: Tourism is Damaging Nature and Itself (Maharjan), 78

Asia-Agriculture: Green Revolution to Gene Revolution (Dixit), 158

The Asian Elephant (Sukumar), 40, 72

Assessing Extinction Rates (May et al), 36

Assessing the Benefits of Bioprospecting in Latin America (Eberlee), 99*

At the Hands of Man: Peril and Hope for Africa's Wildlife (Bonner), 11

Australia: Tourism Gives Aborigines Opportunity for Self-Reliance (Seneviratne), 78

Benign Neglect: A Model of Faunal Collapse in the Game Reserves of East Africa (Soule et al), 40, 41

Beyond 'Participation': Indigenous Peoples, Biological Divedrsity Conservation and Protected Area Management (Colchester), 64, 65, 71, 73

Beyond Rhetoric: Reinvigorating the Struggle for Economic and Social Rights in Africa (Oloka-Onyhango), 24*

Biodiversity and Landscape Management (Naveh), 40, 70

The Conservation of Plant Biodiversity (Frankel et al), 93, 95
Conservation with a Human Face: Conflict and Reconciliation in African Land Use Planning (Bell), 71
Contingency, Irony and Solidarity (Rortyh), 19, 20
Contracts for Biodiversity Prospecting (Laird), 74
Controversial Subjects of Contemporary International Law (Okeke), 166
The Convention on International Trade in Endangered Species (Patel), 129
The Current State of Biological Diversity (Wilson), 36, 37

Deforestration and Indians in the Brazilian Amazonia (Taylor), 54
Diversity Crises in the Geological Past (Raup), 36
Diversity for Development, 159
Do Species-Area Curves Predict Extinctions in Fragmented Forest? (Simberloff), 35, 36
Dying for Ivory (Robinson), 67*
The Dynamics of Extraction in Amazonia (Homma), 76

The Ecological Factors that Produce Perturbation-Dependent Ecosystems (Vogl), 36
Ecological Restoration (Jordan III), 91
The Ecologically Noble Savage (Redford), 56
An Econometric Study of the Causes of Tropical Deforestration (Panayotou & Sungsuwan), 49, 51
Economic Linkages Between Trade in Tropical Timber and the Sustainable Development of Forests (Barbier et al), 13
The Economics of Land and Tilting in Thailand (Feder), 51
Ecotourism, Economics, and the Environment (Tisdell), 77
EECONET and Forests (Voloscuk), 70
An Elephantine Problem, 41
Embedded Systems and Rooted Models (Peters), 52
Endangered Bushmen Find Refuge in Game Park (Daley.), 78
Enola Bean Patent Challenged, 139
Environmental Treaties and Resource Indicators, 109*
Estimating Reductions in Diversity of Tropical Forest Species (Lugo), 35, 38
Evolution and History in Tropical Forests in Relation to Food Availability (McKey et al), 37

ITTO Guidelines forf the Sustainable Management of Natural Tropical Forests, 14
Ivory Markets of Africa (Martin & Stiles), 67*
Jaya Holdings in Deal with Hasko Group, 47
Joint Management of Canada's Northern National Parks (East), 73

Kenya Seeks Way to Save Its Wildlife, 63
Kenyan Wildlife Guards Kill Elephant Poachers, 65
Key Policy Issues (McNamara), 53

Land-Hungary in Brazil (Galano), 52*
Land Resources, Soils and Their Management in the Amazon Region (Cochrane & Sanchez), 50
Land Tenure and Deforestration (Dorner & Thiesenhusen), 49, 53
Law of International Institutions (Bowett), 166
Legal Ivory Trade and CITES (Mathur)*
Legal Mechanisms to Strengthen and Safeguard Transboundary Protected Areas (Shine), 29, 114
Letters from the Amazon (Kane), 58
Living with Wildlife (Kiss), 40
Li ving with Wildlife: How Campfire Communities Conserve Their Natural Resources, 81*
Local Participation as an Instrument of Conservation and Development (Mavenke et al), 80, 83
Local Challenges to Global Agendas (Neumann), 66
Logging Threat Looms Over Birds' Paradise (Chatterjee), 47

Main Report .. Tropical Timber and Sustainable Management of Forests (Barbier et al), 48
Malawi Poachers Pay Dearly, 65
Management of Tropical Natural Forests (Gomez-Pompa & Burley), 13
Managing Global Genetic Resources, 72
Maputo Elephant Reserve Journal, 78
A Matter of Title, 53
The Meaning of Privatization (Starr), 79, 91
A Modern Tragedy of the Non-Commons (May), 37
A Morally Deep World: An Essay on Moral Significance and Environmental Ethics (Johnson), 42

National Parks, Protected Areas, and Resident People (West & Brechin), 55
Native American Mascots, Schools and the Title VI Hostile Environmental Analysis (Trainor), 56
Native North American Almanac (Chapagne, ed), 57
Nature Reserves: Island Theory and Conservation in Practice (Shafer), 35, 72
Neem Tree Patent Revoked, 138*
Neotropical Indigenous Hunters and Their Neighbors (Stearman), 55
Nepal-Culture Winds of Change Sweep Sherpaland (Dixit), 78
Nepal-Energy: Small Hydro-Power Schemes May Save Himalayan Forests (Upadhyay), 78
A New Lease of Life (Reid), 74
New Rules Push Researchers Closer to Biotech Industry (Mudur), 149
Le Nouvel Ordre Ecologique (Ferry), 43

On a Certain Blindness in Human Beings (W.James), 44
On the Nature of Ecological Integrity (Kay), 43
Options for the Coordination of International Action in Forest Conservation and Management (Sargent & Lowcock), 14

Palm Oil Versus Palm Wine (Linares), 56
Panama: Indigenous People Ready to Fight for Land (Hernandez), 55
Parks for Peace, 31
Partners Against Hunger (Baum), 157, 160
People and Parks (Wells & Brandon), 10, 78
People of the Fallow (Balee), 37
People, Parks and Wildlife (Rangarajan et al), 69
The Pharmaceutical Discovery Process (Albers-Schonb erg), 75
Plant Genetic Resources Over Ten Thousands Years (Wilkes), 94
Plant Genetic Resources: The Common Bowl (Kloppenburg Jr. & Kleinman), 135
Plantation Forestry in the Tropics (Evans), 47
Poachers Kill 84 Elephants in Zimbabwe Park, 67
Poachers Killed Five Elephants in World Famous Corbett National Park, 69*
Policies to Control Tropical Deforestation (Barbier & Rauscher), 48
Politicians and Poachers (Gibson), 9
Politics and Histories in Band Societies (Leacock & Lee, eds), 56, 57

Politics, Development and the Indians (MacDonald & Chernela), 55
Poor Farmers Could Destroy Half of the Remaining Tropical Forest, 161*
Preserving Nature in National Parks (Sellars), 39
Principles of Public International Law (Brownlie), 166
Private Conservation and Black Rhinos in Zimbabwe (De Alessi), 86
Private Property Rights to Wildlife - The Southern African Experiment (Muir-Leresche & Nelson), 79, 86
Problems and Prospects for Natural Management of Tropical Moist Forests (Wyatt-Smith), 13, 50
Producing Nature and Poverty in Africa (Broch-Due & Shroeder, eds.), 61
Protecting Nature: Regional Reviews of Protected Areas (McNeely et al, eds.), 70
The Punam: Hunters and Gatherers of Borneo (Hoffman), 56

Rain Forests for Profit (Tangley), 75*
The Reclamation of Derelict Land and the Ecology of the Ecosystem (Bradshaw), 92
Reconciling the Needs of Man and Wildlife in India (Saberwal), 69
Recovery Process in Damaged Ecosystems (Cairns Jr.), 91
Redefining Diversity: Biologists Urge Look Beyond Rain Forests (Anger), 48
Regreening the National PaRKS (Frome), 78
Report on the State of World's Plant Genetic Resources, 94 et seq.
Restoration Ecology: An Acid Test for Ecology (Bradshaw), 92
Restoration Ecology: Ecological Restoration as a Technique for Basic Research (Jordan), 92
Restoration is the Ultimate Test of Ecological Theory (Ewel), 92
Restoration of Degraded Tropical Forests (Hamilton), 91
Rhinos: Conservation, Economics and Trade-offs (Sas-Rolfes), 79
Resident Peoples and Wildlife Reserves in India (Tucker), 73
The Rights of Subordinated Peoples (Mendelsohn & Baxi), 49
The Root Causes of Biodiversity (Wood et al), 1, 47
Rural Poverty, Democracy and Wildlife Conservation (Murphree), 15*
Rwanda-Agriculture (Jaura), 94

S. Africa, Neighbors Sign Cross-Border Park Pact), 16*
Seeds and Property Rights (Swaminathan), 157

# Index

*(Asterisk denotes web site reference.)*